A Prayer Warrior's Guide

How To Pray For People For Divine Healing

A Prayer Warrior's Guide

How To Pray For People For Divine Healing

James Cardona

1ˢᵗ EDITION

I wish to thank my family for their support, especially my wife, Maggie, who is always there for me.

Additionally, I wish to thank George Pace for his valuable contributions of reviewing this book and lifting me up.

As far as thanking people who have contributed to this work, I could really go on listing many names of people for an endless amount of pages as the truth of the matter is that this book is a compilation of so many life lessons that I have learned from a tremendous variety of varied and different people. I thank you all.

A Prayer Warrior's Guide
How To Pray For People For Divine Healing

2nd Printing March 2012
ISBN: 978-0-985-02843-5

1st Printing January 2011
ISBN: 978-0-578-03376-1

Printed in the United States of America
© 2011 by James Cardona

Table of contents

Introduction

"I don't want to die! I'm not ready for this!" she cries out. Pulse pounding, hands trembling, mascara smearing, she can't seem to focus. The phone feels so cold pressed into the hot of her beet-red cheeks. It's too much and all of a sudden. It's happening all too fast. It's the "suddenly" that does it. We can often handle death when it eases in slow and quiet. We can deal with pain if we know it is coming, it is expected. When death fires a warning shot, we lay down our guns and accept it without a fight but this is all of a sudden and out of nowhere. She was altogether fine ten minutes ago, now she is going to die.

She had been taking some medicine for a recent foot surgery and having a bit of abdominal pain. She really didn't like the pain but she tries not to think about it much, she just tries to ignore it, *The belly ache came at about the same time I started the pills so they must be related, right?*

Tired of throwing up almost everyday, she does a little experiment and stops taking the prescription to see if the pain might go away, the throwing up might stop. But the pain doesn't go away. The vomiting doesn't stop. One phone call to her doctor puts her into the emergency room for some tests.

They're just tests, right? she thinks with a mildly increasing panic.

Nothing to worry about, she promises herself quietly.

But it's happening too fast. The rapid series of events is accelerating faster and faster and no matter how hard she slams her foot down the brakes are not working!

After a series of tests and scans she's now no more than a pathetic heap of disheveled mess like a dirty puddle of water left behind by a child's snow boots at the front door. A few hours have passed and her world is suddenly over. This morning she was just thinking about why her boyfriend hadn't called in a few days as she swirled a spatula around to make her eggs just as she likes them, lightly scrambled with a bit of feta and spinach. Now she doesn't know what to think. She can't think; it hurts too much. It's all over. The scan showed a mass in her pancreas that's so large that it's pushing out into the surrounding organs. The pain has absolutely nothing to do with her foot surgery or her prescription. The mass is what's causing all her pain and sickness. She's too afraid to call it cancer, afraid to say it out loud as if it's a big, snarling dog that jumps up barking full blast when it hears its name; she just keeps tearfully calling it "the mass" as she dials the numbers of her closest family and friends that pray, desperately reaching out for anyone or anything that might make this daylight-nightmare disappear.

She has all of the textbook symptoms, it's an open and shut case, no doubt among the surgeons. Her two sons rush to the hospital and one of them brings a medical guide. As he reads off each symptom from the list, her voice becomes lower and shallower each time she is forced to say, "Yes." Eyes clenched down hard, fists in tight awkward balls, finally her voice becomes an inaudible whisper.

They admit her. It's happening too fast. The doctors schedule a final MRI for the next morning and the surgery is to follow immediately after. Apparently the mass in her pancreas is quite large. An endless parade of white coats with silent side-kick nurses with clipboards come in to discuss treatment options, surgery plans, risks, and consequences but all she wants to do is stop and think for just a minute. She wants to breathe for just one solitary minute. She wants to put a stop to time, she needs a pause button for the world. She screams deep inside, "Stop! Stop! Stop!!!!!" but no one hears that voice inside her, nothing stops, her world keeps spinning but it's off kilter, her world is suddenly a child's spinning top that starts to wobble just before it topples over, just before it stops forever.

She calls me right before she leaves to the hospital. She didn't know yet. Just worrying about everyday things, she asks me to pray for her, "Jim, I just need you to pray for me. I want to sell my house and get rid of these dogs. I just need to simplify my life."

She tells me about her foot surgery and feeling sick, but in her voice that is nothing that she's concerned about. We pray for quite a while on the phone and just then I hear God tell me to tell her this, "Your problems are more than physical; they are mental and spiritual. God can heal all three. Jesus can touch every infirmity and every problem."

"Now it is going to happen like this. First God is going to heal your spirit. Then He will heal your mind, then your body. This is

2

God's priority. Watch Him move. If you do not accept the first, you will not get the last. Open yourself up and accept it. Let go and let God. Let God touch your spirit first."

After I hang up, I start to feel a battle coming so I quickly call one of my pastors and the church prayer network is mobilized. I get really nervous about this whole situation which is weird because she really didn't say anything was wrong. She didn't seem worried one little bit, but my stomach is stirring. I start to somehow feel like something is really wrong here.

Others begin to pray about it and a few of the girls go to the hospital to see her. A few hours later I receive a call from one of them who just left the hospital saying that the doctors "found something."

I get out of work late and head straight to the hospital. Worried that I might have missed visiting hours, I bring my Bible and inform the front desk clerk that I came for ministry. Sneering at me in a surprisingly rude way, the clerk says, "Well what are you standing there for? Sign the log-book over there!"

It's when things like that happen that I know some form of spiritual struggle is coming. I politely thank her and move on.

I have to keep myself pure, to keep my heart right, I think. I know the war is already won, it was won on Calvary, but the fight is standing. The battle is standing in faith. The battle is keeping myself right before God.

I enter Room 214A, a typical room with two double beds. If the window blinds were fully open I would have had a nice relaxing view of the helicopter pad and a small open field behind the building that is frequented by deer and rabbits. It is a small room and the adjacent bed is overflowing with a sick mother, her visiting husband and three year-old boy who sound upbeat but pensive. As I enter, the husband politely pulls the divider. The fading sunlight from the window draws their shadows large on the curtain.

The woman's cheeks shine bright red from too much crying as she cautiously smiles an awkward, nervous but hopeful smile. I can see from her eyes that she is happy to see me. The other prayer warriors from church have already been there, prayed with her and left, so she is optimistically hoping things will get better, hoping that she might wake up from all this.

Giving her a few testimonies of other people I know that God had healed, I show her that God could do for her what He has done for others. "God is no respecter of persons," I say, "He doesn't play favorites with His promises. They are available to each and every one of us."

As she opens her ears to what I am saying, God begins to restore her spirit and work on her mind, changing her mind. Her faith is rising up. She is beginning to believe. Her mind begins to change from accepting it as possible to deciding that she can trust God and claim the promise as her own.

We pray right there in front of the two nurses who continually interrupt and the people at the next bed who are trying to ignore us. Let them see God work.

Gradually things seem to matter less and less. All that matters is the relationship with God, the oneness. Nothing else seems to matter. There are no worries or concerns. A feeling showers down on us that God can handle all her problems. In fact, they are not even problems anymore. So small and insignificant, we were looking at them from an airplane window at 30,000 feet. As we pray, the woman rises up, her spirit rises up and she begins to believe.

Then, it's like all of a sudden I know it's time. All of a sudden the time for talking about what God had done before is over. The time for mentally convincing is over. It's time to pray and let God work. God is going to provide faith and move.

Sitting on the edge of her hospital bed, looking down at her toes pointing up through the thin white sheets, I wonder what God is going to do and what will be the result. All it takes is faith but sometimes it's so hard to break through and touch the supernatural. All it takes is the faith of a mustard seed, the tiniest amount of faith, but sometimes we don't even have that. I mutter some words as we pray but it isn't about the words anymore, it's about His Spirit now. He is going to have to do it. God is going to have to come.

He is coming. God is coming, I feel it.

Then, suddenly, God is here. She begins to twitch nervously and cry just a little. She is so distracted that she doesn't even notice her legs moving under the sheet. Something is happening. I don't know what it is, I am just watching now. Yeah, I prayed, I said some words, but so what? They were just words. God's Spirit is here and He is working. He is moving. God changes her mind and her spirit and she will never be the same. All of a sudden she believes she is

4

healed. She knows it. Still sitting in the same hospital bed she was in ten minutes ago yet she is a completely different person in a completely different situation. She is a new person. I see her so different, the faith is shining off her like light. Neither of us knows what is to come, but we both know one thing, she is healed. We have a faith that only God can provide.

We talk for a bit more about other things then I leave to drive home. I continue to pray for her and her situation through the night and it is a constant mental fight for me to hold my faith high, yet I wonder what will happen next and how will God do this? Will she still have to go through the surgery?

The next day, nurses wheel her out and perform the MRI test. She is so confident that she is healed that nothing seems to matter anymore. She smiles at the doctors and even laughs a little. She has Jesus and that's all she needs. She has no idea what the results of the test will be, what the doctors will say or what will happen next, but none of that matters anymore. She has faith in God. She's been touched by the Almighty.

Just before the surgery is scheduled to start, two doctors stumble into her room and one mutters sheepishly, "Sorry but there's been some kind of a mistake, your MRI isn't showing anything. I guess there is no mass."

Unable to explain what's happening he shrugs his shoulders saying, "I guess our first tests were wrong. But funny, I've never seen that before, I mean I know it was there..." He ponders for a second then leaves looking at a chart for his next patient, his face still slightly red.

The mass is gone! God healed her body. By late afternoon, all the symptoms disappear and they release her to go home. God healed her completely.

A few weeks later, She has several follow up checks to verify and she is completely cured. The mass is gone. The symptoms are gone. God completely healed her.

Purpose

There are people that are called to pastor churches, others to spread the gospel through evangelism, and others still that work as missionaries. Likewise, God has called people to pray. I am one such person and this book shares my experiences in praying for people and is written to teach you how to pray and to help you become an expert at praying for people.

Of course, anyone *can* pray and everyone *should* pray, but this book focuses not on prayer in general but on praying for people and getting the results that you are seeking.

So many people pray. Some even believe their prayers will be answered, but how many actually see results? This book will help you get there. It explains how to pray for people who have needs. It explains how to pray for people who have spiritual problems, mental difficulties, and physical hardships. It shows how to pray with results!

Using the principles found in this book, I have prayed for many and seen powerful results. Of course it has not always been this way, It has been a long road to get here and there is still a long way to go.

I was raised a Christian, attended Catholic School and was even an altar boy. As a child, I never questioned whether or not God was real. He always seemed to be there for me with my little concerns, yet I personally never saw anything that I would call miraculous. I never saw anything that couldn't be explained away as coincidence.

Since my father had my sister and I on Sundays after my parents divorced, I spent much of my early teenage years being dragged from church to church as my father tried to find the right fit. One Sunday my Dad hauled us off, sick, coughing and hacking, to another new place, a charismatic church that believed in divine healing. A few short hours later, my sister and I found ourselves in a prayer line, the first that we had seen, much less heard of. I was about fourteen years-old and was healed instantaneously. The flu went away immediately then gradually came back over the next two days.

The sickness coming back couldn't shake the things that I had seen and experienced. I saw the strangest things that day! In a moment God became more real to me than He had ever been before. I suddenly realized that God's promises in the Bible were real!

It has been a long, winding and sometimes crooked road since that first experience, but now, more than twenty-five years later, I have found myself on the other side of the prayer line, praying for people with all sorts of problems, asking God to heal, touch, and deliver.

These experiences in praying for people form the basis of my authority in writing this book. When a person chooses to read something that provides information, many times what is chosen is based upon the writer being an authority on the subject. Many of you, the readers of this book, may never have heard my name before as I am not a person who is part of some "great" ministry. I am just a regular guy who has answered the call of God to pray for people and has spent time crawling through the trenches, getting banged-up, scraped, and bruised along the way and is now sharing those learning experiences.

Having a day job as an engineer, much of my life is bound up in the hum-drum routine of daily life. I am a normal guy, a typical American, who works at a typical company, lives in a typical American home in a typical American town. I am married and have children and much of my family's daily routine is no different than your own. Yet in all my typical-ness, I have experienced the power of God during special moments in my life. It is these special moments that I wish to share with you.

I do not claim to have arrived. I will always be learning, but this book is written to share what I have learned so far. This book is written as a teaching and an encouragement to all the campfire starters that are looking to have effectual fervent prayer in their lives. God can and will certainly bless you with great powerful signs and wonders just as He has blessed me. It has nothing to do with me, the results are not mine but the power of the living God who moved through me just as He will through you.

God is able to touch you in the same fashion as He has done here. I have seen the Lord Jesus heal both the blind and the deaf. I have seen people get up out of wheelchairs and start dancing before the Lord who had no business standing up much less dancing. God is willing and able to touch and deliver.

I am no one of significance in the eyes of this world, yet God has saw fit to allow me to pray using His power and He will do this for anyone who is willing to answer the call. As you will quickly see, God is not partial concerning these promises, they are for everyone, God is no respecter of persons. I am nobody special or significant, everything God has done through me God will do through you and even much more. I humbly submit to you that the great things I have seen and been a part of have nothing to do with me, it was all

God and all for His glory. This great power of God is available to you too.

I have seen marriages restored. One couple that I will never forget walked away hugging each other and crying after walking in with looks of pain, hate, and disgust. This was not due to good counseling, only God can do this. I have seen cancer disappear from people's bodies. I have seen and experienced the power of God. I have seen the Lord Jesus heal deep-seated, multi-year depression. It left in an instant to never return.

The purpose of this book is to help my fellow prayer warriors to pray with results. The purpose of this book is to help you touch those in need, that the Lord God might use you as a yielded vessel to pray for the needy. You might not be a full time minister or even ordained, but God can use you just as He uses me. Everyone is called to pray.

This book is written to equip and strengthen you. This book is to encourage you that you can do it! Answer God's call. Your role is to discover it, to seek God for the revelation of it. Your role is to start functioning in it once you have discovered it. Your role is to grow in it once you have been functioning in it. You can do it!

The purpose of this book is to help you to move forward in what God has already called you to do. Everyone is a part of the whole body and every part is important. Every part has to be healthy for the whole body to be healthy. God is calling us to come together as a body and for everyone to fulfill their part. No one can do it for you. No one can do the thing that God has called you to do exactly in the way that God called you to do it. He is calling everyone of us to pray for each other.

Overview

Each chapter starts with a true personal story and additionally some of the chapters have other stories included in the bodies of the chapters. These stories are not made-up fictions or exaggerations, these events truly happened exactly how I state them. I was actually there. The power of God was on the scene doing the work and I saw it with my own eyes. I am a first person witness to all that God has done here and I am describing these things exactly how I saw and experienced them. God is real. These experiences with God are real. God does not change. Jesus Christ is the same yesterday, today and forever. God still moves in the lives of people today the same as He did back in the days of the prophets and Apostles. This is a first hand account. I am telling you exactly what I saw, felt, and experienced. No more. God does not need me to exaggerate for Him.

Additionally, these stories are not in this book to say, "*Look what I did!*" These stories are for God's glory, not mine. I only happened to be there or maybe to be involved but it was God's power all the time doing the works. In fact, I love to see God work no matter who He chooses to flow through. I am nobody special; you can have an experience with God too. You can pray with powerful results too.

Overall, this book is split up into three sections. The first section describes some of the problems that have gotten people discouraged and stopped them from praying.

The second section provides the scriptural basis for healing and gives the reader foundational material on why prayer works and the Biblical basis for receiving from God. Everyone should know what his or her rights are as a Christian.

The goal is to establish a firm foundation in God's promises for healing and deliverance. If you are going to pray for people you cannot do it with any success if you do not believe that God is going to come through and deliver the healing. If you only think that God *can* heal but may choose to say, "No," then how can you command sickness to flee? How can you lay hands on people expecting them to recover if you have doubt in your heart? So we will establish a basis for our faith and focuses on physical healing. Of course, the blood of Jesus came to give us much more than physical healing but the same general guidelines apply to all other freedoms that we have obtained through His death and resurrection.

We will also look at some of the sources or roots that lead to sickness such as iniquity and generational curses. So much of the hardships that people go through are based upon past history. Sometimes it is past actions that the person had no control over. God can expose the root of these things so that it can be broken and the person healed and restored.

The third section provides a wealth of knowledge and personal experience in how to pray and how to handle various situations when praying for people. We will talk about how to know exactly what God wants you to pray. This is such an important message and has had so little focus. So many times, people will ask for a specific need that is not the *real* problem. There is usually a root and some-

9

times several roots that need to be pulled out. When we pray, we want to do more than cut off the head of the weed; we want to pull it out by the root! So many times people do not even know that this root exists. God can reveal where the true problem lies and how to eradicate it, setting the people free, truly and forever.

Other chapters will analyze some of the reasons why some do not get healed when we pray. We will show how to expose the cause of the problem and show how we, as prayer warriors, can avoid and overcome these issues. Many times the cause can be related to the legalistic way that we think or pray, or a lack of proper preparation or responsibility. Too many times a person walks back to his or her seat in the same or even a worse condition after an altar call. We can avoid this. We can be victorious every time if we are only properly prepared and in tune with God's Spirit of love.

We will also dramatically show how the mindset and responsibility over what God has given us will directly affect how much God trusts us and how much power God places in us. In fact, not only the mindset but the direction of the heart will affect our level of success. Too many are called to pray and yet do not have a heart of love. Certainly there are gifted people who have a level of success but the condition of their heart holds them back.

Perhaps the chapters most dear to my heart deal with power, faith, and authority. I have seen too many people praying in hope, not faith. God responds to faith. To be a prayer warrior you must be intimately familiar with all aspects of faith, not only knowing your own condition and where you stand but being able to see the level of faith in the ones that you are praying for.

Disqualification

Before I close out the introduction, I feel it necessary to assure you that all instruction in this book should be looked at in a positive light. There are sections of this writing that point out areas for improvement and growth. I have made every effort to display them in a positive light but some people may take these types of instruction as criticism and fall into a place of disqualification or condemnation.

Even when God is leading us to new and higher levels in Him, He must show us where we fall short so that we can change. As soon as we see it, we may feel disqualified.

Just recently this happened to me. God was revealing to me things to leave behind, asking me to change in order to grow. Sometimes to grow to a higher level we must leave behind what we are doing now.

When we suddenly realize that we are failing somewhere in our Christian walk, no matter how small and insignificant, we may feel guilty, inferior, condemned, or disqualified. Even though I prayed with authority days before, yet now, because I saw this internal root that had been there for decades, I felt disqualified. When I walked into church that Sunday, a fellow Christian who always prays with me asked me to pray for a man's broken hand. I helped by praying silently but refused to speak as I still had that feeling of disqualification.

Many feel this same heaviness because as the Lord shows what is to be left behind, they might have feelings or attacks that take away their power and authority. We should obviously not feel this way but it is difficult and some arrive at this place. We are all human after all.

One of the risks of writing about areas to improve is that people can be offended or even get this feeling of inferiority or inability. I became paralyzed when this happened to me and even felt as though I could not do what I had already been doing. Yet God will sometimes call for us to change in order to obtain a higher level in Him. Please do not take negatively any areas for improvement that are pointed out. My purpose is for people to grow and improve.

Almighty Father, in Jesus name I ask You to bless these prayer warriors as they start this journey. My dear Lord, open the reader's mind and spirit to new revelation that will strengthen and rise up what You have placed in him or her. Father, look down upon the hearts of Your children and mold them and make them more like You, more like Jesus. Father God, I ask You to glorify Yourself through them. Rise up prayer warriors to glorify Your name.

We give You all honor, glory, and praise and ask these things in the wonderful, beloved, and holy name of the Lord Jesus Christ. Amen.

Section 1:   The Problem

Chapter 1

The Problem

It was dusk on a typical Summer Saturday. On any other Summer Saturday I would be just finishing up cleaning and putting away the barbecue grill or rolling up the backyard volleyball net. My wife and kids would have just gone inside as the bugs are bad at dusk in the riverside town that we live in. But not this Summer Saturday. A friend had convinced me to drive an hour east to attend an outdoor revival meeting in a run-down and depressing park in the middle of a run-down and depressing town that I never had any reason to visit or even drive through mainly because it was run-down and depressing.

My friend didn't show up. The rest of my family didn't want to come. I was in a crowd of four or five hundred mostly Spanish-speaking people from the local area, yet I was alone. I had been milling around for about an hour, not recognizing anyone and wanting to leave but it was the dread of the hour long return trip that kept me there. I didn't want to feel like I wasted so much of my Summer Saturday for nothing.

Standing near the back of the crowd, not knowing anyone, listening to the preacher, I heard something like a whisper in my left ear.

What was that? I thought. It was almost like an echo on the wind. I wasn't sure what it was.

Was that the wind? It was a little breezy, I thought.

I almost thought I heard my name on the wind. Weird. It was as if a distant voice from long ago, trapped in the air, was calling me. Glancing back, I saw nothing but darkness and black everywhere except for a small open area surrounded by tall thin pines where the streetlights still weren't broken.

Maybe it was someone yelling from over on the other side of the park.

I saw some teenagers out there getting high in the surrounding darkness of the park, maybe it was them.

15

Maybe the cars, I thought as I looked at the thin light cast by the headlights of passing cars bouncing between the shadows of the tall pine trees. The drivers were probably too caught up in their daily grind, pondering the day's events and zoning out to the endless radio drone to look over and see what was happening here in the same park that they drove by and ignored everyday. Maybe that noise I heard was coming from those cars.

As I looked around, my eyes kept being drawn to this one lady behind me, sitting way back in the shadows of the trees, all by herself, pressed into a stiff metal chair. I think the event organizers, anticipating the size of the crowd and where the back of it would be, had set up the chair for her earlier, but they were off by about fifty yards. Not as many people showed up as they thought would come. Now she was back there all alone, watching the headlights play tricks with the shadows of the tall pines, watching the neighborhood kids smoke weed, and straining to hear the preacher. As I looked at her, I suddenly knew it wasn't her that called; it was something else. Something in the wind.

I heard it again, more clearly this time. A soft breeze swirling and caressing my ear said, "Go pray for her."

Completely unremarkable, she was the type of person that you glance at and immediately forget. I looked away. Then back again.

Did I really hear that?

She blended into the background yet my eyes were continually being drawn to her. She was just another overweight woman, squeezed tight into a chair and balancing a cane over her left knee. I couldn't stop looking at her; something was telling me to go to this strange looking woman, hiding in the shadows. She had the cane to help her move short distances but she wasn't going anywhere now. She was all alone in that dark corner, resting in a dimming sunlight, straining to hear the preacher, stuffed into that strong metal chair and that was where she was staying.

What is it Lord? Why do you want me to pray for her? I asked in my mind.

I felt the Lord pressing me to go toward her as the night wind swayed the great trees. As I began to walk in her direction, the neighborhood kids began to ease back into the shadows. One of them, the leader probably, glanced at me with the bored look of a lion whose belly was already too full to chase a wounded gazelle.

16

The overweight woman's oversized shirt draped over her too-tight black stretchy pants. Her giant gold earrings hung down to her shoulders. Her feet looked swollen; they bulged out of the tops of her flat shoes. Medical professionals would have called her morbidly obese; her legs were just not strong enough to support her oversized frame for very long.

I introduced myself and asked her permission to pray for her. She agreed.

I commenced praying softly, seeking the will of the Lord. I still didn't know what I was supposed to do or say. I was a bit nervous at that moment. I still was wondering about that wind, *What am I doing here?*

Just then I felt like something was welling up inside of me, pushing up from the inside of my chest, almost like someone just opened a fire hydrant and the pressurized water was bursting out. All of a sudden I *knew* this woman who could barely stand would soon dance. I softly touched her shoulder with the tips of two fingers and started to pray for strength to enter her body.

After about ten minutes nothing had changed, then suddenly her shoulders tensed like she was being shaken from deep inside. It was a great resounding shock-wave of force trembling through her body. Staring at the floor, she squeezed her eyes shut hard. Slight beads of hot sweat formed on the deep creases of her forehead. Something was happening inside of her, the Lord was doing a work and I did not know exactly what it was. I saw another, softer shudder passing through her body like ripples formed on a calm lake. Continuing to pray, I knew it was coming soon. I could feel it breaking. The eggshell was cracking. The baby bird was pecking from the inside.

Just then she grabbed her cane off her knee for reassurance and looked up at me. A momentary wrinkle passed across her face, she gave me a serious look and said, "I feel much better now," then she smiled a sincere smile of appreciation.

She thought it was over. She was thanking me, giving me permission to go away.

Looking at her like a father looks at his daughter as he unscrews the last training wheel, I softly said, "It's OK. Try to stand up and see how that feels."

She paused for an hour-long moment and looked back down at the ground. She had no idea that I would say those words. She had a questioning look in her eyes. Praying is one thing, but expecting a change is something entirely different.

She was hesitant but she tried. She gripped both metal armrails fully expecting the struggle that she had become so accustomed to. She pointed her elbows straight up and slowly edged her weight up onto her shoulders. Then she stood up in one smooth and fluid motion! She burst into laughter full of surprise! Never had she stood up like that, it was always a struggle.

Her eyes were wide open, staring at me in amazement. *Now what?* This was farther than she had ever been. We were in uncharted territory. In this strange and flickering moment I looked at her and smiled. It was as if time stopped for one eternal second.

She started to move forward and test out her new legs. Still gripping her cane but not using it, she gingerly took a few light and cautious steps toward the crowds, leaving me standing there, watching her in amazement. Fading into the background, I felt exaltation as if I had taken that last, final step and was now standing on the summit of Everest. I could only smile. The Lord was working. I was surrounded by a deep silence but I was so close to God. I felt something like the reverberation of the angels cheering on the wisps of the wind in the trees. A sudden gust of wind washed across my ears sounding as if thousands of angelic mouths yelled out their praises for the mighty work God was doing. I was so close. All the praise and worship of the angels was in my ears yet I was surrounded by only the wind in the trees. In my utter awe and amazement at what God had just done, I was disappearing, fading into the darkness of the park.

The music up on the stage was playing now so she started to dance. First a few small steps here and there, then all of a sudden it became so real. Look what God just did for me! She thrust out her legs in two giant kicks and leapt in the air! Prancing like a spry feline charging toward a cornered mouse, bouncing around on her toes, moving confidently away from the shadows and the trees toward the lights and the crowds, this morbidly obese woman danced. She danced!

She didn't need the cane anymore; she swung it in the air over her head. Arching her back, she tilted her head as far as it would go and screamed at the top of her lungs, "Hallelujah!"

Problems

This first section discusses a few of the problems that we face when praying for others in order to describe what we are up against so that we can then overcome it. You cannot conquer your enemy if you do not know that he exists. The second section discusses prayer and healing in a more general sense while the third section addresses the needs of the person who prays for others and builds on the second section's foundation.

This book is written to help everyone, not just pastors or priests. The Bible says that all people are called to attend to the needs of each other, that is, to minister to each other, and one way that we can minister is to pray for each other. Everyone has authority to claim every blessing that is in the atonement. This book applies to all people as all people can and should pray for each other.

Additionally, this book does not discuss prayer in general but praying for others, openly, with the full expectation that God will come and touch. We are going to teach how to pray with results! In Mark 16:17-18, Jesus says:

> And these signs shall follow them that believe; In My name they will cast out devils... they shall lay hands on the sick, and they shall recover.

Most Christians should be familiar with this scripture, yet we see so few people identify themselves with it. This book is here to help all of us walk in it! If we are believers, then let's do what Jesus said we would do. We want to help people with needs just like Jesus did.

Many churches are full of people with problems. These people have physical, psychological, emotional, mental, financial, marital, and spiritual problems and some struggle on like that, day after day, barely surviving. Won't someone pray for them?

In other churches only the pastor or the elders pray and in some cases only because they feel obligated.

Well hopefully God will do something, they think.

Yet nothing changes. I remember the distinct look of trepidation on one ministers' face when a person in a wheel chair rolled down the aisle toward him. A true look of fear stole over his face. He muttered some words over the wheel chair-bound person then quickly moved on.

In other churches, people pray for each other regularly, yet healing and deliverance are less than regular, it only seems to happen some of the time or once in a while. Why? We do the same thing every time, yet some are healed and others are not. What is the problem?

Many times, smaller things are healed but not larger or more deadly. Cold, flu, and poison ivy go away, but those with cancer and incurable diseases go on suffering and eventually die. Why? Can God only heal the little things?

Others seem to feel better for a time after leaving the church, prayer meeting, or revival, yet it doesn't last long. In a few hours or days they are sick again. Sometimes even more sick than when they started.

Maybe it was just my imagination, they think.

Maybe it was psychology.

Yet others receive healing and hold onto it for good. What went wrong?

Some others leave feeling a little better. The prayer seemed to only work a little. Some of the symptoms leave but not all of them.

Well I guess I only had a little bit of faith, so I only got a little bit of healing.

Not all healing is instantaneous, even some of the healing that Jesus did by His own hand was not instantaneous yet everyone He prayed for was healed. We don't have to settle for just a little healing.

Sometimes this lack of success discourages people and makes them reluctant to pray or to be prayed for. It is not that people do not want to be healed, it is just that they do not always seem to get positive results.

Sometimes, there is even a tendency to place blame on someone when there is no success. Why didn't it work? Some blame the person praying saying that they didn't say the right words, they didn't pray right. Others blame the sick person saying they didn't have enough faith or were too full of fear. Others blame God.

Still others take away the parts of God's word that promise healing, freedom, and deliverance saying that it is not promised.

They say, "Well, I prayed right, and that man has been a Christian all his life so he must have faith, I guess it must not be God's will."

20

But it is not about blame. This book is about lifting up you, the prayer warrior, no matter how much experience you have, to enable you to pray with the power and authority of the living God.

Some people have become so convinced that God will not heal that they have developed elaborate theologies around it. These false doctrines have trickled into minds and churches to the point that many people, who do not know where these ideas come from, often quote them, saying things like, "Well you know Paul was sick and God didn't heal him. Remember Paul's thorn in the flesh!"

Yet as we will see, the Bible says no such thing. Healing, freedom, and deliverance are promises from God granted by the atonement and God always keeps his promises.

You will come across many different arguments from people on why divine healing does not, will not, or might not happen. At the same time, we have scripture after scripture that says that God healed people in the times of the Old Testament, Jesus healed throughout the gospels, and God healed using the hands of the Apostles through the rest of the New Testament. Miracles and healing were recorded by the followers of the Apostles and early Christians in the first centuries and this never stopped. Christian history records divine miracles throughout the middle ages and into the Reformation days of Martin Luther and John Calvin in the 1500's, the Holiness days of John Wesley in the 1700's and up into recent times. The great healing revival in the United States from the 1940's until the 1960's saw more people healed of sickness and disease through God's healing touch than had occurred in all the centuries up until that time.[1] God's promise for healing, freedom, and deliverance has never stopped and people are still healed even today. So why do some walk back to their seats still sick or bound up? And why are some so fearful to step out and pray?

I have not met a servant of God who did not want to walk in more power and more authority. Almost every minister wants to serve God more fully. I hear people crying out to God all the time, "Send us Your Rain, send us Your Anointing, and send us Your Power." The whole world groans for a deeper manifestation of the

---

[1] My opinion of course.

21

spiritual and God's healing touch. Yet so many go on with weak ministries, some even powerless. Why?

We are going to answer these questions and more. We will not address each of these questions individually, but will teach how to pray from the ground up. We will start with basics in the second section and then amplify those lessons in the third section. We are going to show you how to succeed in praying for others every time. Jesus said, "These signs shall follow them that believe, in My name they will cast out devils... they shall lay hands on the sick, and they shall recover." Get prepared for this scripture to come alive in you. People will begin to call you a "true believer" because this scripture will become real in your life.

Different than so many books, we are going to de-emphasize step-by-step procedures and instead teach principles. Whenever someone asks you how to do something, what they are really asking for is a series of steps to accomplish the task. The simplest way for a person to think is in a step-by-step procedure sort of way. They have a problem, they want to know how to solve the problem, and they want steps. They want a formula for success. But this is part of the reason people have been failing. Steps will work for some but not all. This book teaches principles, not steps, to help you accomplish the goal of success every time. You will become knowledgeable and confident and will be able to walk boldly to the throne of grace to claim the blessing on behalf of the person you are praying for.

In reading this book you are about to begin a journey. Open your ears, open your mind, and receive with your spirit as God plants a seed of faith in true power. You will never be the same.

Section 2: Healing

Chapter 2

Basis for Healing

It was getting late in the park, only a little more daylight left. The few clouds in front of the fast fading sun formed streaming fingers of light that lit up the gray and blue sky. With no one waiting in the prayer line, I stood at the tent entrance, watching as five seagulls playfully swooped around each other, having fun. Their bodies alternately formed odd hieroglyphics in the sky as they called out to each other. I imagined they were singing about their lives, singing out their joys and pains; the young ones, singing songs from love's songbook, seeking their mates and their futures; the old ones, watching over the young, chirping cautions and recommendations. I wondered if the young ones were listening.

The prayer tents had been slow so far, but sensing the day's end, a crowd began to form. As the next in line entered I left the tent entrance to pray for him.

The old man, partially paralyzed from a stroke two weeks prior, hobbled into the prayer tent. The right side of his body would not respond no matter how hard he tried. And stroke was not his only problem; his legs were covered with great black blotches of skin cancer. Death had given him a one-two punch. As he awkwardly plopped down into the rusty folding chair he gazed up at me slack-jawed with the distant eyes of a man that stared death in the face. I did not ask his age, but his body looked to be made of thick, durable, eighty year-old leather. The deep creases in his skin and the soft look in his eyes spoke to my heart; he was a hard-working man that had lived a hard life. He so reminded me of the men from my childhood neighborhood.

I grew up in a mostly immigrant neighborhood within walking distance of the steel mill in Lorain, Ohio. In the early 1970's business was booming and the mill employed about eight-thousand workers, many of them immigrants. Each street of South Lorain was like a different country. There were Puerto Rican, Mexican, and

25

Ukrainian neighborhoods. There were Czech, Slovak, and Polish neighborhoods, all within a few blocks of each other. Every morning the streets choked with workers walking toward one of the many entrance gates. Life was simple; work hard, provide for your family, and enjoy the simple things in life.

In the summer, many of the families ate dinner on their front porches. I remember the air; thick with the fragrance of ethnic cuisine. I remember being five year's old and running from porch to porch to sneak a taste here and there. I remember the laughter and the simplicity of life. That was all before reality stepped in and stole the dream. The plant shutdown, strike and eventual union lockout destroyed families and lives. The neighborhoods of South Lorain transformed overnight becoming full of broken homes and broken marriages. "For Sale" signs were up but no one was buying. Some of the once-proud workers transformed into depressed drunks or just disappeared, leaving their children fatherless.

This man reminded me of what I saw as a child. He was a simple man, a hard-working man, but life smacked his face and tore his shirt. Now he didn't know what to do. Someone had changed the rules that he had followed all his life.

A Puerto Rican, he wore the traditional Guayaberra, a pair of well-worn blue work pants, and black mesh slip-on sandals that had a small hole where his left big toe could peek out.

He had walked in cautiously; slow and steady. It was a walk of reverence and respect as if he was crossing the threshold of the inner court into the holy of holies. He stared at the ground as he tip-toed in.

He demonstrated his illness for us. The right side of his body was mostly paralyzed. He could barely raise his arm as he strained to use his shoulder muscle, only about two or three inches, no more. Once passed that point, excruciating pain shot through his entire body. An involuntary hiss slipped past his lips as his body shuddered and his knees buckled from pain. The arm itself was paralyzed and unusable; it was dead, hanging meat.

At first, I didn't know how successful we would be as he didn't speak much English. Any person can pray, but sometimes you must lift their faith. Faith is the key. Sometimes, you have to show them what is promised and convince them so they can receive and we couldn't understand each other. We couldn't communicate.

He did not respond to anything much we said except to say, "I got Jesus."

Over and over, he kept saying, "I got Jesus."

What he meant was that he had already accepted Jesus as his savior although it took us a while to figure that out. Several of the prayer warriors looked at each other in frustration. *What could we do?*

My Spanish was marginal and this man had a thick accent that I was having a hard time understanding. We refused to just say some words over him and send him on his way, hoping for the best. We wanted to get it right but we couldn't communicate.

Finally a Spanish language translator arrived. We began to communicate with him and lift up his faith.

Face full of sorrow, the paralyzed man could not understand why he was afflicted. He felt like he had done right all his life, he went to church, he paid tithes. For him, this was a curse. He couldn't understand how a good person who was trying to do right could be afflicted with something like this.

"Why did this happen to me? Why am I cursed? Why is God punishing me? It doesn't make sense!" he exclaimed.[2]

The shell on his face broke. A change stole over his face, the attitude of "why me?" rushed out. His face cracked like an egg shell and thick tears poured down his cheeks. He cried out for forgiveness. A long, painful, guttural scream shook the tent. As his wail died out stillness eased into the space.

Then Jesus came.

The Holy Spirit descended upon this man for the first time in his life and he was healed instantly. It was an instantaneous healing. It was like lightning. He did not shake, he did not shudder, he was just healed. Sliding off the metal chair, landing on his knees and ele-

---

[2] Sometimes people can only understand a little. Do not think that you will be able to explain everything to everyone. Do not think that you can show everyone everything you know or see. All you need to do is give them that one nugget, that one mustard seed. (Matthew 17:20) All they need is a mustard seed of faith and the mountain will move. Give them that mustard seed and you will see great miracles.

vating both arms above his head, he screamed at the top of his lungs, *"Gloria! Gloria! Gloria!"*[3]

His voice bounced off the trees and echoed through the park. He was healed! All signs of paralysis were gone. Death was knocked off the wagon, trampled by the horses, and drug under the wheels.

The single light bulb hanging from the corner of the tent seemed to flicker brighter somehow. The prayer warriors started dancing, hollering, and praising God! People leapt into the air and flailed their arms, punching the sky with victory jabs. The screams were so loud that people from all over the park craned their necks to see. I glanced outside and the people waiting in line for prayer were staring, mouths open, in bewildered amazement. They couldn't speak, only stare. They had seen the man that had gone in. They knew he was paralyzed; now he was dancing!

The man's body shook and trembled from the anointing power of God's Spirit, his frame was in a spiritual earthquake. His body was shivering so hard! He had goose bumps all over. Power was reverberating through him. He became strong. He became mighty!

So excited and full of victory, he begged us to allow him to pray for the others. "I want to pray for them," he said with a trembling voice in broken English as he pointed toward the remaining people in the prayer line.

As he began to pray God started healing through this man's touch. He went to those just outside of the tent, those still in the prayer line. As he touched them, there was a noticeable transfer of power; God was using this man to heal. The man who came in had a body full of death. The man who walked out was a minister of life.

Healing Basis

This chapter lays out a scriptural basis for healing in order to help mentally convince people that healing is available. Additionally, it provides a simple and basic explanation of how faith is developed. In later chapters we will get into much of the new meat that has inspired me and additionally we will further dissect the process of faith in order to understand the principles of how it is developed.

---

[3] "Gloria" is Spanish for "Glory."

Faith is the necessary element, without it, your prayers will not produce results. We must have faith.

Before someone can receive divine healing there is sometimes a need to first understand the Biblical basis for it. Sometimes, they have to be reassured that healing is promised for them. Other times they have to be taught that it is even possible. This chapter will outline one scriptural proof to mentally convince people that healing is available to them.

Convincing people that God will heal is sometimes the biggest part of the battle in praying. The proof in this chapter is only an example of one such proof, there are many other ways to teach people this truth and as you gain experience you will begin to see which direction to proceed with people.

In our proof, we will start off by saying that Jesus healed when He was on earth and since God does not change, then God certainly still heals people today. Next we will see that God does not play favorites in who He chooses to heal, God will heal anyone who approaches Him in faith. Finally, since faith is the approach, we will briefly talk about how to develop faith for healing.

Too many people know too little about the Bible, yet a few things they seem to know is that God can heal but *only if it is God's will* or that Paul had a "thorn of the flesh" that God did not heal.[4] The truth is that physical bodily healing is promised for those who believe. Physical bodily healing should be expected every time.

There are many scriptures that promise healing and these scriptures should provide the basis for our faith. In this chapter we are going to build our case for healing upon the promises that God gave in the Bible.[5]

God does not change

Our proof starts off simply. God healed in the times of the Old Testament and New Testament. Everyone knew that Jesus was a healer. Even the Pharisees did not discount His works. Jesus was

---

[4] We will talk more about Paul's "thorn" later.

[5] Note that in harder cases you sometimes cannot use this approach as some people believe the Bible has been corrupted over the years or that the Bible is not fully inspired. They will say things like, "Well the Bible was written by men." Do not give up in these situations. God will still work. You just have to be more flexible.

recognized far and wide in His day as a healer and that is one of the reasons many people flocked to Him.

Today, many people believe in a historical Jesus, but does Jesus still heal? Yes! If Jesus healed two-thousand years ago then he will do it again today. Hebrews 13:8 says:

> Jesus Christ the same yesterday, and today, and forever.

And Malachi 3:6 says:

> For I am the Lord, I change not.

The works that Jesus did two-thousand years ago can certainly be performed by Him today. Jesus does not change. God does not change. Everything God has done, God can still do. God healed in the past, God can still heal. If Jesus ever was a healer then He still is a healer. God does not change. Jesus does not change. If God ever was God then He is still God.

Additionally, the very nature of God is to heal. God called Himself a variety of names in the Old Testament besides Y_HW_H. Some of the other names He called Himself described His Nature. For example, He called Himself Jehovah-Jireh which means *I am the Lord that provides*.[6] He also called Himself Jehovah-Rapha which means *I am the Lord that heals*.[7] He used these titles to describe Himself and tell us who He is. He was describing His own nature when He gave Himself these titles. So it is in the nature of God, a God who does not change, to heal.

If you worked as an engineer, you would have no problem telling people, "I am an engineer." It is who you are and what you do. God said, "I am Jehovah-Rapha, I am the Lord that heals." It is who God is and what He does and God does not change.

All who approach Jesus are healed

The power of God will heal all ailments. There is no affliction so foul that it cannot be healed by God. There is no problem, whether emotional, physical, mental, or spiritual that God cannot handle. God can touch all.

---

[6] See Genesis 22:14 for the use of the title *Jehovah Jireh*.

[7] See Exodus 15:26, Isaiah 53:4, and Matthew 8:17 for descriptions of God as a healer, *Jehovah Rapha*.

In Matthew 4:23-24, we find:

And Jesus went about all Galilee, teaching in their syn-agogues, and preaching the gospel of the kingdom, and healing all manner of sickness and all manner of disease among the people.

And His fame went throughout all Syria: and they brought unto Him all sick people that were taken with di-verse diseases and torments, and those which were pos-sessed with devils, and those which were lunatic, and those that had the palsy; and He healed them.

And in Matthew 12:15, it says:

But when Jesus knew it, He withdrew himself from there: and great multitudes followed him, and He healed them all.

Also look at Matthew 8:16-17:

In the evening time, they brought unto Him many that were possessed with devils: and He [Jesus] cast out the spirits with His word, and healed all that were sick: that it might be fulfilled which was spoken by Isaiah the prophet, saying, "Himself took our infirmities, and bare our sickness-es."

In Mark 6:56, it says:

And where ever He [Jesus] entered, into villages, or cit-ies, or country, they laid the sick in the streets, and sought Him that they might touch but the border of His garment: and as many as touched Him were made whole.

You might start to notice from these examples that Jesus healed all people of all diseases and cast out all demons of people who were *brought to Him.*

Of course there are Biblical examples where Jesus heals only one person out of many. In the following example many people were sick and Jesus walks up to one, the one who had faith, and healed only that one and left. John 5:1-9 says:

Some time later, Jesus went up to Jerusalem for a feast of the Jews. Now there is in Jerusalem near the Sheep Gate a pool, which in Aramaic is called Bethesda and which is surrounded by five covered colonnades. Here a great num-ber of disabled people used to lie—the blind, the lame, the paralyzed. One who was there had been an invalid for thirty-eight years. When Jesus saw him lying there and learned

31

that he had been in this condition for a long time, He asked him, "Do you want to get well?"

"Sir," the invalid replied, "I have no one to help me into the pool when the water is stirred. While I am trying to get in, someone else goes down ahead of me."

Then Jesus said to him, "Get up! Pick up your mat and walk." At once the man was cured; he picked up his mat and walked.

Now I want to make a distinction here. There is clearly a difference between the times when Jesus *went to* someone to heal them, and when the sick *came to* Jesus. When Jesus went to someone, He sometimes only went to one person —the one who had faith. On the other hand, when we come to Jesus, He heals all of us of all of our sickness, and casts out all demons. Our coming to Him is the exercise of faith. It is faith that is the key.

Here is another example of Jesus healing all of the people who came to Him. Luke 4:40-41 says:

Now when the sun was setting, all they that had any sick with diverse diseases brought them unto Him; and He laid His hands on every one of them, and healed them.

And devils also came out of many, crying out, and saying, "Thou art Christ the Son of God."

And He rebuking them suffered them not to speak: for they knew that He was Christ.

Before we say that divine healing only happens when Jesus prays, let's look at Acts of the Apostles 5:12, 15-16:

And by the hands of the Apostles were many signs and wonders done among the people; (and they were all with one accord in Solomon's porch.

Insomuch that they brought forth the sick into the streets, and laid them on beds and couches, that at the least the shadow of Peter passing by might overshadow some of them.

There came also a multitude out of the cities round about unto Jerusalem, bringing sick folks, and them which were vexed with unclean spirits: and they were healed every one.

The power of God will heal all ailments. There is no problem beyond God's reach. His arm is not too short. The power of God will heal all people that have faith and approach Him to be healed.

God does not play favorites

OK, so God *can* heal and we have seen that God does not change. So then God still heals today. Also we have seen that Jesus heals all people of all diseases and cast out all demons of people who approached Him requesting healing.

But is He willing to heal me?

Yes, God does not give healing specially to one person over another. God treats all people equally. God does not play favorites. In Acts 10:34-35, Luke writes:

> Then Peter opened his mouth, and said, "Of a truth I perceive that God is no respecter of persons: but in every nation he that fears Him, and works righteousness, is accepted with Him."

Since God treats everyone equally, God must treat all of us the same when we request healing. If one person receives healing by approaching God in a certain way and another person approaches God in the same manner, then the second will receive healing likewise. Romans 2:11 says:

> For God does not show favoritism.

And in Ephesians 6:9 Paul writes:

> ...you know that He [God] who is both their Master and yours is in heaven, and there is no favoritism with Him.

God does not change and God does not play favorites. It is written in Colossians 3:25:

> But he that does wrong shall receive for the wrong which he has done: and there is no respect of persons."[8]

Again, if approaching God in a certain way has healed a person then God is obligated to heal us if we use the same approach. It is His Word! God said that He is not partial and He treats everyone the same! Obtaining healing is not God's choice, it is ours. If we

---

[8] Deuteronomy 10:17 also says that God is not partial

approach God in His provided way then He is obligated to heal because God does not play favorites. He treats us all the same.

Faith is the Approach

Now, we have quickly seen that God *can* heal and that healing is in the nature of God. It is who He is! Likewise, we have seen that since God does not change and God healed in the past then God must still heal. Jesus Christ is the same yesterday, today and forever.

Also we have seen that God does not play favorites. Therefore if we approach God in the same manner as another who has received then we **must** receive likewise. God is no respecter of persons. If we use the same approach then God is obligated by His Word to treat every person in the same way.

Obviously there are many cases of people being healed by God so all we need to do is approach God in the same way that they did and we will receive likewise. Knowing how to approach God will defeat the enemy every single time.

We have seen that Jesus heals all people of all diseases and cast out all demons of people who approached Him requesting healing. So, *how* do we approach? The approach to healing is always through faith. Faith is the necessary element. It is faith that touches the hem of Jesus garment, not any step-by-step procedure. We must have faith.

Remember, faith has nothing to do with the five senses. Faith could even be called a sixth sense, a spiritual sense. In fact, in the case of healing the five senses *may* run counter to faith. I have seen many people who are seeking after healing who visually look at their symptoms and if the symptom does not immediately get better, they lose faith. Or sometimes the symptoms get better for a few days, and then later get worse.

They say something like, "I thought for sure God would heal me!"

Clearly these people did not understand how faith works and therefore they opened the door for the disease to return. Here is an example of what one person wrote me:

> I want this evil affliction to leave me. I want to have a healthy life. I hope someone will join me in prayer. To hear the Lord is a Healer right now is such a distressing statement for me because I

can't understand why I have not been healed all these years and why I am allowed to suffer like I was still doing my old evils. Healing is the children's bread right? Why is it not being served to me? I know the Lord loves me but if only He could heal me. Please pray with me.

I love this brother but this is a perfect example of wrong thinking. The Lord God *can* heal anyone. The Lord *wants* to heal, it is in His *nature*. Everyone *can* receive healing, they only have to *believe*.

So, how do we believe? How do we know when our faith is sufficient? How do we obtain an amount of faith necessary for our healing?

So far we have given a very brief scriptural basis for healing, now let's take a moment to talk about the mechanics of faith and how faith is developed. Again this is a simple and basic introduction, in later chapters we will address the dynamics of faith in greater detail.

Faith is a Process

Obtaining spiritual faith can be described as a process. First, we must hear about the thing that we are to believe in. How can we believe in a thing that we have never heard of?

Second, we must make a mental choice to accept what we heard as true. We must take it into our minds and believe it mentally. Many Christians do this but never go past this point. Be careful! This is not yet true faith! Third, the Holy Spirit must come and reveal it to your spirit. The Holy Spirit must provide the faith.

Before we elaborate on this process of developing faith in greater detail, let's differentiate between the two different kinds of belief that we can talk about: the mental–psychological kind and the spiritual kind. Often there is confusion between these two because the way that people use language is not always rigorous and exact. So then let's add at least a little rigor to our definition of the terms "faith" and "belief" as we move on.

When most people say that they "believe" something, what they actually mean is that they "think" it is true or a fact. Since people use the term *believe* to mean *think*, we are going to call this phenomenon a *mental belief*. This mental kind of belief occurs when we choose to hold something in our mind. It is actually a choice or a mental agreement. When we choose to believe something, we are making a conscious decision that what we say we believe in is true. This is often called *mental ascent* or *mental agreement*. So then, in reality, a mental belief, as I have just defined it, is not faith at all, but a mental choice.

Our second kind of belief is not mental at all; but spiritual. This is the true faith that is described in the Bible. Only the Holy Spirit can give true spiritual faith. True faith, as we will see in later chapters, is something tangible and spiritual. It is not a thought or a choice. It is something real.

People can be preached to, or read the Word, and say that they believe something in the Bible because it sounds good and makes sense. Maybe it is reasonable because it is the same message that they have heard since they were small kids. But do they believe it *truly*? Or is there a shadow of a doubt? So many times people say, "I believe such and such..." when what they truly mean is, "I think such and such..."

Is there only a mental belief or is there also a spiritual faith? Spiritual faith only comes through the Holy Spirit.

Hebrews 2:2a says:
 Looking unto Jesus, the author and finisher of our faith...

Jesus is the author of our faith. God provides faith. God must place the faith inside of us. We will amplify this concept in a later chapter but for now let's look at this process of obtaining faith.

First :: Hear

Before the Holy Spirit can come, a person must first accept mentally. The Holy Spirit is not going to fall on an unrepentant sinner and *force* him or her to be saved or to be healed. Furthermore, before a person can choose to accept something in his or her mind the person must first have heard about it. Hearing about it is the very first thing that must happen. Romans 10:17 says:
 So then faith comes by hearing, and hearing by the word of God.

And Galatians 3:2, 5 says:

> This only I want to learn from you: Did you receive the Spirit by the works of the law, or by the hearing of faith?
>
> Therefore He who supplies the Spirit to you and works miracles among you, does He do it by the works of the law, or by the hearing of faith?[9]

Hearing is the first step in the path to faith. The words that we hear enter our minds and then we must make a choice.

Second :: Choose

In order to develop a mental "belief" or accept something mentally, we must make a choice. We must choose, in our minds, to believe it. We must choose, in our minds, to accept the thing as fact. We must "get our minds out of the way," as I call it. Later, the Holy Spirit will come and give us a spiritual belief. The Holy Spirit will come and provide faith.

The person who wishes to be healed must convince himself or herself mentally that God will give personally what He promises in the scriptures literally. The person must rely totally and completely on the promises of God found in the scriptures, not on any change in physical symptoms. Once this happens, he or she now has a mental "belief." It is accepted in the mind as a fact.

If you have already read other fine authors who write about topics of faith you may already be familiar with this form of mental belief.[10] Often this form of mental belief is decried as inferior to true faith (which it is) but still it is a necessary step on the road to true faith. God will not step past your will. This mental choice is our second step and is necessary because we must choose, but it is not yet true faith.

Third :: Believe

Now we have completed the first two steps; we have made a mental choice to believe that God will take away our infirmity. Next

---

[9] Notice that the first quote says that faith comes by hearing while the second quote says that we receive the Spirit of God by hearing. Hint. Hint. More on this in later chapters.

[10] Many call it *mental ascent* to avoid using the words "faith" or "belief" when describing something that is only in the mind and not yet in the spirit.

we must believe spiritually. A mental choice or metal belief is not enough, we must receive faith and faith is only provided by God. Jesus is the author and finisher of faith.[11] God provides faith. So how does this happen? How do we open ourselves up to God so that He can come in and plant a seed of faith deep in our spirit?

In order to allow God to enter in and provide spiritual faith, we must first get rid of anything that would block that entrance. We must free ourselves from any mental disbelief. We must get our minds out of the way. We must flush out those shadows of mental doubt that are lingering in the back of our minds. This may sound contradictory since two paragraphs above we just said that we already had a mental belief, but in fact, there are generally lingering doubts, sometimes buried deep in the mind.

We must free our minds from any shadows of doubt and allow God to enter in and provide a spiritual seed of faith. Prayer helps to free the mind. Pray and ask God to honor His Word and His promise to us. Of course the mind is very tricky. That shadow of a doubt can be lurking deep down in the back of the mind.

Is this real? Is this really going to work? Will God honor me when I am a sinner? What have I done for God?

These thoughts, jumping in and out of the head, come from two different places. Some are attacks of the devil. The devil has many thousands of years practice at disrupting prayer and faith.

Other times people sincerely have doubt. They have little or no experience with faith so there is uncertainty. In either case, the mind can get in the way. The mind has to be clear of these doubts, uncertainties, and attacks before faith can rise up.

People receiving cannot worry about mental attacks. They cannot pay any attention to them. When you pray for people, suggest that they let go of their five senses and focus on the Word. They should not consider anything but the promise of God. Help them to keep their mind's eye on the promise found in the scriptures only. Pray, pray, and pray some more. They should meditate only on those scriptures and remember to claim the healing. It often helps to have them say the words instead of you speaking for them. What you are actually doing is trying to get their mind "out of the way" so that the Holy Spirit can come.

---

[11] Hebrews 2:2

38

Do this for as long as it takes. Sometimes it takes a few moments, sometimes several hours. If you have to take a break and pick up the next day, OK, but never leave this subject until the blessing is received. Do not give up early –pray for as long as it takes. In Luke 11:5-8, it is written:

And He [Jesus] said unto them, "Which of you shall have a friend, and shall go unto him at midnight, and say unto him, 'Friend, lend me three loaves; for a friend of mine in his journey is come to me, and I have nothing to set before him?'

And he from within shall answer and say, 'Trouble me not: the door is now shut, and my children are with me in bed; I cannot rise and give thee.'

I say unto you, "Though he will not rise and give him, because he is his friend, yet because of the man's boldness he will rise and give him as many as he needs."

After a time, the person's mind will "get out of the way," that small shadow of a doubt will leave, and the Holy Spirit will come and provide spiritual faith. When that happens the body may or may not still have the physical signs of the sickness. The disease or ailment may leave instantaneously, or it may not. There may be some physical sign of the healing or there may not.

But regardless of the condition of the body, once they receive faith, the person will **know**, without any doubt, down in the depths of their spirit, that they are healed. This is revelation knowledge – the true spirit of faith that can only be granted by the Holy Spirit. It will not matter what their eyes see before them, they will **know** that they are healed. This is true faith and true faith is only provided by God.

Tell them to hold fast to that revelation and if the healing was not instantaneous then after a time the body will respond.

Understand that the devil will start to attack the mind but rebuke him using the Word. Remember Abraham who did not consider (look at) his age or the deadness of Sarah's womb but only considered (looked at) the promise of God that he would have a son in his old age. Romans 4:19 says:

And not being weak in faith, he [Abraham] did not consider his own body, already dead (since he was about a hundred years old), and the deadness of Sarah's womb.

39

It is not that he denied that he was old –he knew he was old – but he looked at the promise of God anyhow. He held fast to the promise –God's Word. He stared at the promise and didn't blink.

Tell them to keep holding onto that blessed revelation that they are healed. Do not let their mind get back "in the way." Do not listen to the evil one. It is fine and all right to check and see if symptoms are still there, but tell them to not look at any change in symptoms to prop up their faith. Even if it looks like they are getting better or they start feeling better, encourage them to continue to focus completely on the promise, not on any change in symptom. Their faith should be only in God's Word.

Do You Want to Believe?

Many have no experience with faith, they have never experienced true, Holy Spirit provided faith before. They cannot recognize it. They do not know if what they already have is enough. Receiving this Holy Spirit provided faith is the hard part. So many people stop at a mental belief or a mental acceptance of what is promised and they are just not there yet. That's OK, just help them to get to the next step, help them to pray for the faith and the Lord will provide it. In Mark 9:23-24:

Jesus said unto him, "If you can believe, all things are possible to him that believes."

And straightway the father of the child cried out, and said with tears, "Lord, I believe; help my unbelief."

And we find that Jesus did help his unbelief, and the child was healed. Jesus both provided the faith necessary for the healing, then performed the healing. You see, sometimes we want to believe so badly but we don't know if what little faith we have is enough. The man said he believed, but also recognized that his faith was small, there was some doubt. *Will God honor this little bit of faith that I have?*

Remember, Hebrews 2:2a says:

Looking unto Jesus, the author and finisher of our faith...

God provides our faith. We can never believe enough mentally. Making a choice in our minds is just not enough. We must have a spiritual faith and God alone provides that faith. Believing in our mind is not faith at all but just thinking. Faith is something spiritual and is in our spirit. It is a *knowing* deep down in our spirits, not in our minds. Jesus is the author of all faith. God provides faith through the work of the Holy Spirit and there is no amount of thinking alone that will work. It is through faith and faith alone that miracles happen.

If we are trying to pray for people with results, we must become masters at helping people to get their minds "out of the way" and false ideas out. We must become masters at showing them and teaching them the Word concerning healing so that their minds might accept it. We must learn to recognize and discern the difference between a person truly believing and having spiritual faith and a person who says, "I believe," yet it is all mental thinking.

Healing is one of the promised guarantees that we received through Jesus' shed blood on the cross. This chapter was a brief introduction into the scriptural basis for healing and the process of developing faith.

So far it may seem as though we are giving steps in describing our faith building process but this is solely because we are building a simple framework. We will continue to explain the principles of faith in greater detail in later chapters which will allow us to move away from any step-by-step procedures and toward fully developed principles.

Now that we have an introductory foundation in the Biblical basis for healing we will move on to a simple foundation on how to pray. Later we will talk about why some people do not receive healing and how to break though in these situations.

Chapter 3

How to Pray

The realization struck like the blasting horn and blinding light of a freight train, like the belching exhaust of hot air from the speeding engine; something was deadly wrong. Something that I had known about but not considered important was now the most deadly serious thing in my entire life.

I had been bleeding a little bit more each day but I never thought much of it. It had been going on for about a month, but it was just a drip or two, here and there. It was nothing that I even thought about twice. I knew it was there but thought it was nothing. Now a painfully deep realization smashed me in the face and took my breath away, I stood up and the toilet was full of blood.

I felt heartbeats reverberating through my skull.

What?! Why?

The palpitations were so loud. Like a large, dull, sand hammer pummeling both temples of my skull, it was so loud I could barely concentrate. I could barely focus on anything but the deep red.

Squish. Squish. Squish. Squish.

It was a peculiar sound in my head. I don't know why I was focusing on the sound right at that moment but it had such a squishiness to it. I was staring at all my life, just like all my blood, all in the toilet, yet I was all so fascinatingly distracted by this squishy sound in my head. I think I was hearing high-pressure blood being squeezed through the suddenly too-small veins in my brain. My heart was pumping *so* hard.

Squish. Squish. Squish. Squish.

I couldn't think. I just stood there with my pants around my ankles, starring at the blood and listening to this new amazing sound. My legs felt weak and rubbery; I leaned back against the bathroom countertop for support.

Squish. Squish. Squish. Squish.

I felt the cold air on my skinny legs as my leg-hairs stood up at attention.

A million thoughts raced through my mind like a host of hornets scrambling from a just knocked-down nest.

Why is this happening to me? I'm so young! Is this a curse? What have I done wrong to deserve this!

Squish. Squish. Squish. Squish.

Have I disobeyed God somehow? I don't deserve this! Is it cancer? How much life do I have left? What do I do now?

The thoughts bounced around my head stinging the side-walls of my skull on every landing. I couldn't seem to focus on anything except the blood. I had tunnel vision. The periphery became a blur.

Squish. Squish. Squish. Squish.

"There are only a few causes for this and one of them is colon cancer," I thought morbidly.

All of a sudden I felt like it was all over. It didn't matter how long I had been a Christian and how strong my faith was, fear was jumping all over me. Maybe it is just human nature but my mind leapt to the worst-case scenario; cancer. I am not a *negativo,* I am usually positive and upbeat but death was staring back at me with swirling, blood red eyes.

I always told people that I wasn't afraid to die. Over and over I told people that I had no fear of death.

"My salvation is secure," I said confidently.

"I know where I am headed," I boasted.

But this was real! This was the real-deal, right now, staring at me, right back at me, right at my face!

"What do you say now?" the blood seemed to ask.

As I stared at the blood and the minutes passed, my body shuddered hard as I finally asked myself the question that I had been dodging, "Am I afraid to die?"

The question hung still in the air. It was the nine-hundred pound elephant in the room, pressing me hard against the wall, that I was trying to ignore. I knew that I didn't really have an answer.

After about half an hour I got tired of staring at the blood and not being able to answer that question. Pulling up my pants, I left the room not knowing what to do. I knew I couldn't move forward, couldn't do a thing, until the question was answered.[12]

At first I didn't tell anyone, not even my wife. It was the question that was driving me. I was completely distracted. I only responded to people in a whisper and quietly looked away. As the day wore on, my mind began to drift off to explore. Who was I *really*? What did I truly believe? The questions.

I had to know the truth, not just trying to convince myself that I believed. I needed to know what was real, what were the facts. It was far too late to lie to myself and try to fabricate some absurd fantasy just to calm myself down. This was real. I was going to die, at least I truly thought I was, and I had to know the truth, the real truth.

As I began to seek answers, my spirit responded.

My faith was solid; I was *not* afraid to die. If I was to die in the near future then I knew where I was headed and it was OK. I was at peace with it. I truly knew, in my heart of hearts, where I was headed. I was a Christian. I believed. I was headed to heaven, if not now, then someday. I would be alright. When I was gone God would take care of my family, just like he has done for others. I had nothing to worry about. Peace increasingly came over me the more I contemplated it.

It is extremely difficult to be healed through faith when your sole motivation is fear. To run to Jesus for healing because you are afraid to die just doesn't work. It is the wrong motivation. I knew that I had to get rid of the fear first, then I could move forward, so after a time of soul searching and contemplation, I decided I wanted to be healed of this. I knew who I was. I was a believer. I wasn't going to go crying to God because I was afraid to die. I was moving forward in faith, not fear.

My wife has always been a cautious woman and she loves me; she forced me to make an appointment for a colonoscopy after I told her about the blood. I knew I would be healed, I could feel it, but I agreed as long as they would "only look." No cutting allowed.

---

[12] Hebrews 2:14-15 says that when we have "fear of death" that we are slaves to the devil. He controls us: "Since the children have flesh and blood, He [Jesus] too shared in their humanity so that by His death He might destroy him who holds the power of death—that is, the devil— and free those who all their lives were held in slavery by their fear of death." (NIV)

The specialist's office was booked up for three months but after describing my condition, an emergency appointment was made. I was losing too much blood. The doctor was very concerned and placed me on the emergency list. He would put me under and go in with his instruments in three days.

With God all things are possible and easy, but with man there can be difficulties. I have seen too many people try, fail, and give up too early. When doubt comes into their minds, they lose faith. You have to be prepared for battle because the demons are going to fight you over every inch of ground, every inch of your mind. Sometimes it is not even so much any sort of outside evil, but the lack of experience that you may have. Many people don't need any outside force to make them doubt, they do it all on their own.

To be free from doubt you have to know what you are promised in the scriptures, and know that they are the true Word of God. You have to know that this faith thing is really going to work or you can't begin to use it.

As the blood flow increased, I stuffed wads of paper and rags in my pants to sop up blood. I didn't want to ruin my clothes. I didn't want others to see it. It was dripping out constantly. By the next day I was perpetually light headed. I had lost too much blood. I was weak and tired. It was weird to me that even my brown skin began to look grayish and dead.

As I continued to pray, I analyzed myself. Did I have anything that would block my healing? Is there anyone that I had not yet forgiven? Is there anything that needs to be made right? I knew I had to take care of these things first. I didn't want the devil to use them to attack me mentally and try to block my faith.

"Make things right first," I thought. Many times all it takes is a phone call.

My blood flow was progressively increasing. On the night before the procedure the intestines must be flushed out. I could not eat for twenty-four hours and had to drink a nasty tasting solution that gave me instant and prolonged diarrhea. As I drank the solution I pondered how I would make it through. I was already light-headed from the loss of blood, now I was going to flush out much more.

I had been praying since it started but now I was in the showdown. I felt the tension in the air of an old western shootout in a

Sergio Leone movie.[13] It was high noon and I was facing off with a demonic gunman at the OK corral. The dust blown street was empty of all but tumbleweeds. On either corner we stood, facing each other, eyeing each others' guns. A dry silent tension was in the air. No one moved; no one flinched. Who would fire first? Who would be left standing?

I had prayed for so many people that received healing; it wasn't like I didn't believe. I knew God wanted to heal me, but this time it was *me*. I saw people healed of cancer before but it was always someone else. I was never the one that was sick. I was always somehow disconnected. It was never *my life* that was in jeopardy. It was never *my life* hanging in the balance. When I finished praying for someone I was always headed back to my routine, business as usual. It wasn't me that was gripping down tight to just hold on.

I didn't leave the bathroom for several hours. I couldn't, the turbo-lax flushing solution they gave me was too strong. I eventually took all my clothes off and locked myself in because I was tired of stripping down every three to five minutes.

In the short time between each flush I found myself peering into my own eyes in the mirror, looking into my own spirit. The reality of life and death stared back at me. I saw my own mortality. I saw my short life and how little it meant. I saw the things that I had wasted time on. I saw how stupid my priorities had been.

The muffled sound of my children playing came through from the other side of the door. They had no idea. Would they still have a father in two weeks time?

I looked at all the things that I thought were important just three days ago and such a disdain ran though me. I felt like I had wasted so much of my life on things that were so pathetically unimportant.

I paused for a moment when I heard a dripping sound. I thought it was the toilet leaking but it was me. As I stood there, the blood was dripping out, splashing onto the tile floor between my feet. A puddle was forming. Suddenly I realized that there would be no tomorrow. It was now or never. I would never make it to the doctor's office tomorrow. I was bleeding out.

---

[13] Sergio Leone was an Italian film director probably most well known for his westerns that featured Clint Eastwood.

As I refocused, staring into my own eyes in the mirror, my mind flooded with voices, distracting me from praying, telling me I was about to die, laughing. They were so loud! They wouldn't shut-up! There was a constant drone of voices yelping in the background of my head. I couldn't think.

I began to pray in earnest. This was it. It was now or never. It was the showdown.

I asked God to heal me. I asked for it based upon His promise.

I cried out, "Lord Jesus, in your Word, I see that *all* people who approach You in faith are healed. Lord, according to your Word, I know that You *are* a healer. Lord, according to your Word, I know that You *can* heal. Lord, according to your Word, I know that it is in Your *nature* to heal. You called Yourself Jehova-Rapha. Lord Jesus, according to your Word, I know that You *want* to heal."

I began asking God to give me what He has already *promised* to give. It was not that I deserved it because I didn't. I was leaning on His promise.

I continued, "You said, 'Ask, and it shall be given you; seek, and you shall find; knock, and it shall be opened unto you.' So, I am coming to You, Lord, by faith in the promises found in Your Word and asking You to heal me as You have promised.

"You said, 'The prayer of faith shall save the sick, and the Lord shall raise him up.' I am basing my faith totally and completely on Your promise found in Your Word. I will not place my faith in any change in my symptoms, but only in your Word. "

I continued praying like this for about thirty minutes. At first it was desperation but later I felt my faith start to rise. I fell into a kind of a trance as a hazy cloud of glory surrounded me right in my bathroom. I don't know if it was real or just my eyes being blurry from the tears but I began to slowly forget about my other concerns. Things of the world just didn't seem so important anymore. The babbling voices in my head drifted reluctantly yet softly into the distance. Like the dull haze on the horizon of a setting sun, I was all of a sudden drifting in eternity, alone with Jesus. It was so peaceful there. Nothing seemed to matter, not even time, or space, or distance. My life was as nothing. I just wanted to stay there, drifting in the cloud, for eternity.

Just then a realization struck me. As I came out of the trance I had a supernatural faith that I was healed. I *knew* that I was healed.

The Holy Spirit touched me. He placed a spiritual knowing deep inside of my spirit. It was a revelation. I *knew* it. It became a part of me.

Once the revelation came, I felt like I had an authority over the situation. I felt like an army commander in full charge of a battle platoon. I was in charge! I turned my attention to the sickness and commanded it to leave. I opened my mouth and directly addressed it.

"Sickness, according to the promise of God found in the book of James, you must leave. It says, 'The prayer of faith shall save the sick, and the Lord shall raise him up.' I have prayed in faith and therefore you have no choice but to leave this body. I am speaking on the authority of the Lord Jesus Christ. Sickness, I rebuke you. Sickness, I cast you out in the name of the Lord Jesus Christ. You have no choice but to leave. You have no authority here. You are commanded to leave in the name of the Lord Jesus Christ."

It felt so good. I felt so powerful. I knew the sickness had no choice, I was full of God's authority. It was not just saying those words and hoping everything would turn out all right. I *knew* everything was fine, I *knew* God had me in the palm of His hand. The Holy Spirit provided this knowledge supernaturally. It was a spiritual revelation.

I began worshiping God and thanking Him for healing me. I was so confident. I was so happy. There was yet no external evidence but that didn't matter. *I knew!* I Praised God's holy name and claimed the healing.

I said, "According to Your Word, I am healed! Thank you for healing me, Lord Jesus!" I praised and praised and praised.

I put on my clothes and triumphantly came out of the bathroom. From across the room I announced to my wife that I was healed; I didn't need to go to the doctor.

She immediately became visibly upset, "Well, I don't care what you say! You are *going* to that doctor tomorrow!" She had just put the kids to bed.

I paused for some moments and thought of her heart and her love for me. I answered softly, "No problem. I'll go, but the doctor will not find anything. You'll see."

Of course, I knew it was always perfectly all right to check my symptoms but I would not put any faith in them. My faith was totally and completely in God's Word.

Sometimes the healing will be a process. We might start getting a little better initially. We might start *feeling* better. It is very tempting to fix in our minds that, "Look! It's working! I'm starting to get healed!" I knew not to do this because what I would actually be doing is starting to rely on my feelings or a change in my symptoms instead of relying on my faith in the Word. This is a big mistake. I relied on my sixth sense not my five senses. Regardless of what the doctor said, I relied on my faith not my feelings. What I have seen is that sometimes people turn their attention away from the Word and towards their feelings when things seem to be working. Then if there is a negative change in the feelings or symptoms, they lose faith. I refused to do that. It was all right for me to check my symptoms, but I would keep my faith totally and completely on God's Word.

Just after my wife and I spoke, I felt another flush coming on. I quickly shuffled off to the bathroom barely making it to the toilet. Every previous flush had been a deep, dark red, full of more of my life, more of my blood. I stepped over the puddle on the floor. It was still there, in my excitement I hadn't yet wiped it up.

This time there was the smallest drop of blood mixed in with the water. Just one drop, no more. Every flush after that one was completely clean and clear. It was a miracle; God healed me.

The following day, I went in for the procedure and gave explicit instructions to the doctor that he only had permission to look with his camera, nothing more.

When I awoke from the anesthetic, he showed me a picture of what looked like a bruise on my intestine.

He said, "I don't know what this was, but it is healing up now. You will be fine."

But I already knew that.

Step by Step

This chapter provides a brief framework on how to pray for others in three simple steps. As you will see later, I do not believe in using step-by-step formulas or procedures when praying. In fact, it would be absurd to provide a step-by-step formula for prayer and say that **everyone** who does a set of steps will get healed. Yet, when the people asked Jesus how to pray, He certainly told them what to do and what to say. So just as Jesus showed us how to pray using the example of the "Our Father" prayer yet He was really teaching principles, we will give three steps, not as a procedure but as a framework for learning principles.

In an ideal world, the people you are praying for would not have any strongholds or areas of disbelief. They would not have any "spiritual baggage." In an ideal world, they would not have any past hurts and offenses to deal with. They would simply believe and receive when you prayed for them.

In an ideal world, people would be able to tell you exactly what they needed. They would actually know what the problem was and know what direction to pray.

This has actually happened for me a few times but generally this is never an ideal world. There are almost always a whole host of other things to deal with. Before we address some of these other things, we will use this chapter to speak on how to pray in the almost non-existent ideal situation.

We will be using three short steps, but understand that this is only a general framework. The goal of this book is to teach principles, not formulas and procedures. You will see in later chapters a more perfect and comprehensive way to operate. Just as Jesus gave us the "Our Father" prayer[14] and yet we so often use different words as the situation warrants, the outline of "how to pray" in this chapter is just a conceptual guide –a place to start.

We have previously seen that God *can* heal and that healing is in the nature of God. Likewise, we have seen that God does not change and God honors any person who approaches Him in His pre-ordained pattern. If we approach God in the same manner as another who has received then we **must** receive likewise.

Also we have seen that Jesus will heal **all** people that have faith and approach Him to be healed. We have seen that before the Holy Spirit can come and provide faith a person must first believe mentally. We have looked at some scriptures to boost our mental "belief" and we understand that the Holy Spirit alone provides faith.

Next we must pray and ask God for the healing. The thing to remember is that there is no time element with prayer. The moment that we pray, our prayers are heard and the floodgates of heaven are opened.

---

[14] Matthew chapter 6

Of course there are some things that can block your prayer, such as being unrepentant, unforgiveness, or a lack of faith, among others. We will look at some of those later.

Be Specific

We must be specific in what we pray for. Pray for exactly what we want and believe that we will receive exactly what we ask for. Psalms 27:4 says, "One *thing* have I desired of the Lord, that will I seek after..." We must fix in our mind what we desire. Pray for that exact thing and expect to receive that exact thing. Seek after this one thing until it happens.

Now, the promise from God that is written in His Word is that if we pray we will be healed. In James 5:13-16, it is written:

Is any among you afflicted? Let him pray. Is any merry? Let him sing psalms.

Is any sick among you? Let him call for the elders of the church; and let them pray over him, anointing him with oil in the name of the Lord: and the prayer of faith shall save the sick, and the Lord shall raise him up; and if he has committed sins, they shall be forgiven him.

Confess your faults one to another, and pray one for another, that you may be healed.

The effectual fervent prayer of a righteous man avails much.

This is the Word of God now. It said, "And the prayer of faith shall save the sick, and the Lord shall raise him up..." It does not say that the Lord *might* raise him up. It does not say the Lord will raise him up *only if He is in the mood*. It does not say the Lord will think about it first and then say, "No." It says, "The prayer of faith shall save the sick, and the Lord shall raise him up!" Here are a few more scripture quotes that might help. In John 14:13, Jesus says:

And whatsoever you shall ask in My name, that will I do, that the Father may be glorified in the Son.

Also in Luke 11:9-13, Jesus says:

And I say unto you, Ask, and it shall be given you; seek, and you shall find; knock, and it shall be opened unto you.

For every one that asks receives; and he that seeks finds; and to him that knocks it shall be opened.

If a son shall ask bread of any of you that is a father, will he give him a stone? Or if he asks for a fish, will he for a fish give him a serpent? Or if he shall ask an egg, will he offer him a scorpion?

If you then, being evil, know how to give good gifts unto your children: how much more shall your heavenly Father give the Holy Spirit to them that ask Him?

In Mark 11:20-24, it is written,

And in the morning, as they passed by, they saw the fig tree dried up from the roots.

And Peter calling to remembrance said unto Him, "Master, behold, the fig tree which You cursed is withered away."

And Jesus answering saying to them, "Have faith in God.

For verily I say to you, that whosoever shall say unto this mountain, 'Be removed, and cast into the sea';

and shall not doubt in his heart, but shall believe that those things which he said shall come to pass; he shall have whatsoever he said.

Therefore I say to you, what things so-ever you desire, when you pray, believe that you receive them, and you shall have them."

At the end of Mark 16:17-18, Jesus issues the great commission to spread the gospel to the entire world and says:

And these signs shall follow them that believe; In My name shall they cast out devils; they shall speak with new tongues; they shall take up serpents; and if they drink any deadly thing, it shall not hurt them; they shall lay hands on the sick, and they shall recover.

Again, this is the Word of God. This is Jesus speaking! He said, "They shall recover." Jesus does not say that they *might* recover. It does not say they *sometimes* recover. It says, "They shall recover!"

Three Steps

Many people have asked me to explain *exactly* how to pray for healing. They are not sure if they should beg at the feet of Jesus or demand to be healed. On the one hand it sounds like we have no faith and on the other it seems like we are ordering God around.

Again, these steps are a simple framework. In the big picture this is not about formulas, it is about faith, authority, and thanksgiving. So this is just a framework to get us started.

This framework can be divided into at least three distinct parts: ask God for healing, command the sickness to leave, and then thank God for the healing; faith, authority, and thanksgiving.

Ask God for Healing

First, we ask God for healing. We do not command God. Neither do we beg, but we ask God to heal based upon His promise that He gave us. We are only asking for God to give us what God has already promised to give us.

Say something along these lines, "Lord, in your Word, I see that all people who approach You in faith are healed. Lord, according to your Word, I know that You are a healer. Lord, according to your Word, I know that You can heal. Lord, according to your Word, I know that it is in Your nature to heal. You called Yourself Jehova-Rapha. Lord, according to your Word, I know that You want to heal."

Continue, "You said, 'Ask, and it shall be given you; seek, and you shall find; knock, and it shall be opened unto you.' So, I am coming to You, Lord, by faith in the promises found in Your Word and asking You to heal me as You have promised. You said in your word, 'the prayer of faith shall save the sick, and the Lord shall raise him up.' I am basing my faith totally and completely on Your promise found in Your Word. I will not place my faith in any change in my symptoms, but only in your Word. "

Speak Directly to the Sickness

The second step is not really a prayer at all but is really speaking directly to the sickness or demon. Once faith comes, you have all authority to cast that thing out.

Turn your attention to the sickness or the demon and command it to leave. Say, "Sickness [Demon], according to the promise of God found in the book of James, you must leave. It says, 'The prayer of faith shall save the sick, and the Lord shall raise him up.' I have prayed in faith and therefore you have no choice but to leave this body. I am speaking on the authority of the Lord Jesus Christ. Sickness, I rebuke you. Sickness, I cast you out in the name of the Lord Jesus Christ. You have no choice but to leave. You have no authority here. You are commanded to leave in the name of the Lord Jesus Christ."

Now, some people will scream loudly and get very excited and emotional. That is all right to do that, but it is not necessary. It is not emotion that is scaring the sickness or demon into leaving but it is the power of the name of Jesus being used in faith.

Thank Him for the Healing

The third part of this framework is praise. Worship God and thank Him for the healing. Praise God's name and claim the healing.

Say things like, "According to Thy will and according to Thy Word, I am healed!" and, "I am healed according to Thy will Lord!" and "Thank you for Healing me, Lord Jesus!"

Repeat scriptures. Say, "The Bible says, 'What things soever you desire, when you pray, believe that you receive them, and you shall have them' and I believe that I receive, Lord!"

Block the Return of the Sickness

Now encourage people to get full of the Holy Spirit to prevent the sickness' or demon's return. Tell them to never open the door to Satan. Tell them to never stop praying, never stop reading the Word, and never stop seeking after holiness, purity, and righteousness. In Luke 11:24-26, Jesus says:

> When the unclean spirit is gone out of a man, he walks through dry places, seeking rest; and finding none, he [the demon] says, "I will return unto my house whence I came out."
>
> And when he comes, he finds it swept and garnished. Then goes he, and takes to him seven other spirits more wicked than himself; and they enter in, and dwell there: and the last state of that man is worse than the first.

If the person has not obtained the Holy Spirit in his or her heart yet or hasn't kept a continual filling, then a door is left open for the demon or sickness to return. In John 5:14, it says:

Afterward Jesus found him in the temple, and said unto him, "Behold, you are made whole: sin no more, unless a worse thing come unto you."

Again, these three short steps are merely a general framework. We are now going to move on to discuss some of the causes of sickness and some of the barriers to receiving healing such as generational curses and iniquity. In later chapters, we will return to more fully develop our framework that we began here and we will see more clearly how to be led in exactly what to say and do when we pray for others. We are going to briskly step away from any legalistic, step-by-step, procedural mindset to move into the principles of faith and authority in order to carry out the will of our Lord Jesus.

Chapter 4

Iniquity and Generational Curses

Hesitating to stand up and walk to the altar, he finally just slumped back into his chair, watching everyone else go forward. His mind drifted as he looked down and away in that comfortable defeat that he knew so well. Suddenly uninterested in what was happening around him, he studied the veins on the back of his hands like a scientist viewing a new species for the first time.

He was a simple man, a practical man. He was a man who came as he was. Button-down, short-sleeved, Florida shirt; white cargo shorts and open-toed sandals; he wore his everyday clothes to church. As you saw him was as he was, no pretending with him. And there was a certain masculinity about him, he looked like one of those men you see in your neighborhood who are abnormally comfortable doing the brutal work of shingling roofs in the pounding summer heat. Yet he was more than all that; he was a spiritual man.

He knew God was real, he had been touched before, yet so many times he prayed and nothing happened. So many times others prayed for him and his situation had not changed. He was hesitant, he didn't want false hope again. Beat-down from excessive praying with little or no results, He was frozen in his chair, falling into a sullen series of stupid little distractions. He still wanted a real God with real results, but just didn't know how to reach Him.

I saw him treading water, lost in a bottomless sea of trouble, a sea that had no shore. It was like he was bobbing up and down with the waves, squinting at the endless horizon, no shore in sight.

He wanted prayer, he wanted to be free of the disease. He hated being an alcoholic. He fought against it with everything he had because it was destroying his life, it was destroying his family. That clear, seductive fluid only dealt out pain in the long run.

Once upon a time he loved it, it was a dear friend, always there for him. They had fun, they sang and laughed together. Slowly the relationship changed. He became like a battered wife who keeps

57

coming back hoping that her husband would change, hoping that the lies and the hitting would stop, hoping that it would eventually be all better, that it would be like it used to be in the beginning.

No, he detested that poison. He hated it but still thought he couldn't escape it forever. He had gone long spells without a drink but in his mind it was as they always say, *"Once an alcoholic, always an alcoholic."* Even if he went years without a drink it stayed with him. He had to stay ever vigilant, ever watchful. Never let your guard down! As soon as you slip once its all over! The slope is too slippery. The slope is too steep.

Once he tried to end it. In a drunken and depressed stupor he threw a rope over a limb on the backyard tree and tied it around his neck in a poorly made noose. He fell off the chair and began to hang. There was no sudden jerk, his neck didn't break but he couldn't breath. He bobbed and bounced in the air as he started to get weak, the life was slowly draining from his body. As the rope squeezed tighter and tighter, he gasped. He struggled a bit, but he was hammered-drunk, there was no way he could get himself down, the chair had fallen over.

Just then his young son ran into the backyard. He ran up to his father and stopped right in front of him, hanging from the tree. His son didn't know what was happening at first. The boy stood a few feet away and looked up into his paling face. He stopped bobbing and shaking. He stared down into his young son's face. It was his own face thirty years earlier that looked back at him. As their eyes met, their gaze locked, the Holy Spirit spoke.

Instantaneously he was sober. The Holy Spirit took away his drunkenness. He saw his son. He *really* saw his son. The drunkenness was gone. He saw reality. He saw the horror in his son's eyes. He saw what the drink had done to his son. He saw the impact on all he truly loved. He watched as the knife of alcohol cut his son's mind. He watched as the scar was forming before his very eyes. He could never undo it. The history of his life was laid out simple and plain before him, he saw the hurt and despair.

His wife ran out and cut him down and the drunkenness returned, but the experience changed him. It was then that he decided to be free, whatever it took.

He never wanted to return to those days of the drink. His wife and kids had suffered too much. He had real problems and he wanted a God that was real. He was not going to get prayed for and fake some kind of shaking or falling down to make everyone feel like they did something good. He needed to be free. He didn't need the hype.

A group of us men went to him at his chair. Something in the way he sat there, slumped over, staring at the floor, called us. As we prayed for him, I began to seek the Father asking Him what to do, what would happen, where He was taking us. I knew God could set him free in a moment, but many times God wants to do things in a certain order. Many times God has a different set of priorities than man.

After about ten minutes, I felt in my spirit that he was going to be set free. It was as if I was somewhere else all of a sudden, like I was on the water, sailing, and my spirit was the sail, spread out wide to catch the wind of revelation. My spirit was spread and stretched taunt, pushed by the strong east wind of God.

It would not be "once an alcoholic, always an alcoholic, and no more drinking." No. He would be free. So many people never drink again but still have that curse of desire hidden away deep inside of them. It is like an internal force waiting for an opportunity to destroy. No, the man would never long for the bottle again. The internal desire for the alcohol would be completely removed.

Just the thought of that freedom brought tears to my eyes. I began to weep like a child. It was that unknown emotional kind of cry where you can weep for hours and not know what you wept for. I was about to see God's glory right before my very eyes.

The other three men laid hands on him and prayed. I stood back; I was so shaken that I could barely open my mouth. A strong anointing flowed. I felt something deep happening. He started to sob. The men were involved in a complicated and intricate dance, it was unchoreographed, unrehearsed, yet each move was delicate and precise. Something was being drawn out of him, it was the beginning of a metamorphosis. The chrysalis was cracking open; the butterfly was beginning to emerge.

A few minutes later he stood up, looked all around with surprised eyes, and bolted for the back door. No one knew why.

Once outside he began to vomit in the bushes. It was a deep retching, a purging. He wasn't even nauseous a few moments earlier, now something from the depths of his belly was screaming to come out.

As he vomited, it all came out. Out went the pain, out went the despair. Each wave of retching pulled out something deeper.

Out went the misery, out went the guilt. He heaved and heaved as it all poured out. His stomach was a raging rapids, boiling and tumbling over river rocks.

Out went the hurt, out went the sorrow. Something deep inside of him was coming out and it wasn't food. It was the desire. Out went the desire! God changed him internally. God removed the desire for the drink. No matter if he sees a billboard or an open liquor store there is no desire. No matter if someone drinks in front of him and even offers him a drink there is no desire. No matter the temptation, there is no desire inside of him! God removed the desire!

Generational Curses

The following chapter goes into two related subjects: healing of the soul (mental or emotional healing) and generational curses. Many times when people ask to be prayed for it is not for a physical sickness but for an emotional or mental problem or the removal of a desire such as smoking, pornography, or vanity. Other times the person is physically sick but it is the desire or some form of curse that is the cause of the person's problems. The person may be physically healed but until the root is removed he or she will never be truly free. This chapter reveals the Biblical promises for freedom from generational curses, freedom from desires, and emotional healing.

Generational curses are curses that can be upon a person based on what was done in previous generations. Many times whole families say they have *bad luck* or never seem to have anything "go their way." We are going to see that there is a Biblical explanation for this and there is a Biblical way to break through this problem.

Additionally, many times this generational curse comes in the form of a sinful nature or tendencies toward a sin. Alcoholic fathers seem to have alcoholic sons for example. The nature or tendency toward the sin can actually be a generational curse.[15] Of course this is not always the case, but freedom from these problems is available regardless if they were caused by generational curses or not and therefore we will spend part of this chapter talking about this type of healing.

---

[15] Some scientists have claimed a genetic link in family behavior patterns. We do not know if this is has anything to do with generational curses in the Biblical sense.

What is a Nature?

Here are dictionary definitions of *nature* and *spirit*:

Nature: The inherent character of a person,
          An inner force in an individual. A behavior.

Spirit: The activating principle influencing a person,
          A special attitude or frame of mind: *the money-making spirit was for a time driven back.*

The nature of a person is the behavior of the spirit of the person. The spirit inside of a person is what drives the behavior or the outside actions. So then, the unseen, invisible spirit of a person causes the seen, the nature, or outward behavior of the person. The two are different but tied together because one is the thing itself and the other is the action of the thing.

For example, we can say that a person who is born in the United States and acts in a patriotic fashion has an *American spirit* or *a spirit of American patriotism.* So the behavior is an outward sign of the inner spirit.

Especially evident in families, we can find some people that have almost the same nature, behavior, or way of looking at things. They yearn after the same things and think alike. As the old sayings go, "The apple does not fall far from the tree" and "Like father, like son."

These sayings capture something that we all observe: that many children act just like their parents or other family members. Immediately we think that this is due to upbringing, genetics, or maybe environment. Of course, these factor have an influence, but almost all of us can think of a person who grew up to be just like a family member who did not live in the house. A child who is *just like* his uncle, father, or grandfather, *who he never met.* How can this be?

Let me give you one example of this. One single parent told me that her "bum husband abandoned her" when her child was only a few months old. The father was never seen again. He was a heavy gambler and a glutton. Of course, the mother raised her son as best she could and did not expose him to any of these vices, yet he turned out just like the father he never met. Even to the point of mannerisms, ways of talking, smiling and joking. Yet, he never once met the man. How can this be?

Well, it's because our nature is dependent on more than just biological factors, genetics, environment or upbringing. We have a spirit and at least part of our nature is based upon our spirit.

So then the spirit inside a person influences the behavior of the person and the spirit of a person can be affected by the actions of his or her parents and grandparents due to generational curses or blessings. This "spirit nature" is passed down from generation to generation, even among family members that might have never met. In Exodus 20:5, it is written:

> You shall not bow down yourself to them [false gods], nor serve them: for I the LORD thy God am a jealous God, visiting the iniquity of the fathers upon the children unto the third and fourth generation of them that hate Me;

And in Exodus 34:7, it is written:

> Keeping mercy for thousands, forgiving iniquity and transgression and sin, and that will by no means clear the guilty; visiting the iniquity of the fathers upon the children, and upon the children's children, unto the third and to the fourth generation.

Here is another translation of that same passage:

> Showing grace to the thousandth generation, forgiving offenses, crimes and sins; yet not exonerating the guilty, but causing the negative effects of the parents' offenses to be experienced by their children and grandchildren, and even by the third and fourth generations. (Stern's Complete Jewish Bible)

So, according to the Bible, if a parent or grandparent is bad, God will *visit* this iniquity onto the children in that family. Counterwise, if a person is good, God will *visit* this blessing on to the children in that family.

So what is iniquity? And how do we become free from it? Just because Uncle Tony was a drunkard, does his little son have to become one too?

Iniquity

Iniquity is a difficult term to define. The etymology of the word says it means *uneven* or *unequal*. One dictionary says it means *absence of moral or spiritual values.* So, most people have taken this to mean *sin*. And in a way it is. But the Bible clearly uses both of the words *iniquity* and *sin* in addition to the word *transgression*, so there are different shades of meaning.

We are going to describe iniquity as a *sin nature*. This sin nature causes people to desire to sin. Remember our definition. A nature is an inner force in an individual that is seen outwardly as a behavior. These people are born leaning toward a certain type of sin. This inner desire, this iniquity, is placed on the children of a sinner as a curse because the sinner did not repent when God called for repentance.[16] If they are children of gamblers, they might be born with a desire for gambling. This predisposition toward the sin is iniquity and it is a curse.

Freedom from Iniquity

Each of us has some form of nature and we can cover it up or run from it, yet the internal desire is still there, the iniquity is still there. We can bury it deep, never to surface, yet it is still there. We cannot free ourselves, by ourselves, from ourselves.

Thanks be to God, we can be free from iniquity just as much as any sin. We cannot do it by ourselves, but with God nothing is impossible. In Isaiah 53:5, several characteristics of the messiah's mission are described:

> But He was wounded for our transgressions; He was bruised for our iniquities: the chastisement of our peace was upon Him; and with His stripes we are healed.

An interesting point about this passage is that the external wounds were for physical healing because "with His stripes we are healed" and the internal injuries were for freedom from iniquity be-

---

[16] God does not immediately place a curse on someone. First God tries to give a person direction. If they ignore God's direction, He will correct using chastisement. If that doesn't work, then God will rebuke. If that doesn't work, then the sinner becomes cursed. There are many layers to God's instruction and He treats us just like a good father would treat his most precious children.

cause "He was bruised for our iniquities." Iniquity is an internal sin nature. The Lord Jesus was bruised internally to free us from this internal curse and heal us internally.

Iniquity is a spiritual desire for sin that can be placed on people and passed down onto later generations, but we can be free from it. We can be free from any curse that is in our family. We can break the cycle.

When Nature Has Conceived

James 1:15 says:

Then when nature has conceived, it brings forth sin: and sin, when it is finished, brings forth death.

The sin nature is not the sin itself, but the thing inside that causes a person to *want* to sin. It is a nature that "brings forth sin." Of course, everyone has free will and can choose to not listen to that little voice inside crying out for that vice. Just because you have a sin nature, does not mean you have to listen to it. "The devil made me do it" is never a valid excuse. But still you can be free from the sin nature, God can remove that little voice that calls you toward something that you do not want to do.

Another illustration of this iniquity can be found in the typical presentations given at meetings such as Alcoholics Anonymous. People take turns standing up and saying things like, "Hello everyone, my name is such-and-such and I am an alcoholic. I haven't had a drink in ten years." So even though they no longer drink, they acknowledge that the nature is there, the desire to drink is there, the internal longing is there. The person hasn't had a drink in ten years yet is still considered an alcoholic because it is not the outward behavior that defines him or her but the internal desire. That is what God can remove. He can free us from the desire for the sin. He can take away the longing for it.

Some people say that, "Once you are an alcoholic, you are always an alcoholic," even if you do not drink for ten years. When God is done removing the addiction to alcohol, you would say, "I am not an alcoholic, I am free from it!"

Jesus' Bruise

Now let's look at the Biblical explanation for how exactly we can become free from iniquity. As we have already said, it was by

Jesus receiving internal bruising. Now remember what we are talking about is mental, emotional and psychological bruising not a physical, bodily bruise because iniquity is not physical but in the mind, in the psyche. This mental bruising occurred at Gethsemane.

First, know that the symbols in the Bible have a direct relationship to what they represent. For example, Jesus received bodily damage to take on our bodily ailments. He took on physical "stripes" to give us physical healing. Likewise, he took on psychological "bruising" to give us freedom from internal iniquity and we can be free from any sin nature or any mental, emotional, or psychological problem because of this bruising.

We know that Jesus took on death through the crucifixion and we know that He took on physical "stripes" when He was whipped and scourged by the Roman soldiers. But when did He take on this internal bruising of the soul?

Jesus was "bruised for our iniquity" in the garden of Gethsemane,[17] prior to His capture by the soldiers. Let's revisit this story and look closely at the events that take place right before He arrives at the garden so that we can see the full story of how this freedom was given. We will open up the story at the Last Supper, reading in John 13:

> 2 And supper being ended, the devil having now put into the heart of Judas Iscariot, Simon's son, to betray Him...

A little later, Jesus says:

> 18 "I speak not of you all: I know whom I have chosen: but that the scripture may be fulfilled, he that eats bread with Me has lifted up his heel against Me."
> 21 When Jesus had thus said, He was troubled in spirit, and testified, and said, "Verily, verily, I say unto you, that one of you shall betray Me."
> 25 He then lying on Jesus' breast said unto Him, "Lord, who is it?"
> Jesus answered, "He it is, to whom I shall give a sop, when I have dipped it."
> And when He had dipped the sop, He gave it to Judas Iscariot, the son of Simon.

---

[17] The word Gethsemane directly translated means "oil press." The garden was an olive grove and olives are pressed or crushed to remove the olive oil. Gethsemane was the place of Jesus' crushing and pressing.

And after the sop, Satan entered into him [Judas]. Then said Jesus unto him, "What you are going to do, do quickly."

30 He [Judas] then having received the sop went immediately out: and it was night.

Therefore, when he [Judas] was gone out, Jesus said, "Now is the Son of Man glorified, and God is glorified in Him."

What is happening here at this moment in the Last Supper is that Jesus is giving permission to the devil to kill Him. Prior to this significant event, the devil only had limited permission. The devil was held back. Many times the Pharisees or town's people tried to kill Jesus [being driven by the devil], but He "slipped away."[18] Now, Jesus gave the devil and all his army permission to place their full arsenal of spiritual warfare against Him. Jesus gave them His permission to torment, attack, and destroy Him.

Notice that Jesus also says; "Now is the Son of Man glorified, and God is glorified in Him." He was not yet crucified, yet Jesus clearly states that now it has happened.

The fulfillment of Isaiah 53 takes place over a period of time which includes multiple events. [19] It begins from this moment at the last supper and carries on until the moment that Jesus is hanging from the cross and says, "It is finished." [20] Many people focus only on the cross yet the bruising, the stripes, and the cross are all tied together.

Continuing with our story, after the last supper Jesus goes to the garden of Gethsemane to pray. He has an unseen army of darkness piling up misery on His mind, His soul, and every ounce of His being. They can now do this because of the permission He has just recently given to them. Matthew 26:36-39 says:

Then came Jesus with them unto a place called Gethsemane, and said unto the disciples, "Sit here, while I go and pray yonder."

---

[18] John 5:13, Luke 14:47, Mark 14:49, John 8:59

[19] Isaiah 53 is one of the prophecies of the coming messiah, it describes many of the messiah's attributes and freedoms that he will bring.

[20] John 19:30

And He took with Him Peter and the two sons of Zebe-dee,[21] and began to be sorrowful and very heavy.

Then said He to them, "My soul is exceeding sorrowful, even unto death: wait here, and watch with Me."

And He went a little further, and fell on His face, and prayed, saying, "O my Father, if it be possible, let this cup pass from Me: nevertheless not as I will, but as You will."

Some people have focused on this statement, "Let this cup pass from Me" and said that Jesus did not want to die. They say that the "cup" is the cross. Not so. The cup was all the iniquity of the entire world. The cup was the internal bruising that He was receiving. He was drinking the cup of the world's sorrows and consuming it internally.

Jesus had the full weight of the entire world's iniquity bearing down on His soul. He was "exceeding sorrowful, even unto death." He had great depression, great woe, great anguish, and great misery. When a person becomes excessively depressed and miserable, it is not long before he or she might want to die. The darkness becomes unbearable. Depression can become so great that death looks like a path to freedom from it. Jesus had so much misery due to this great burden of the entire world's iniquity. To say that He wanted to avoid the cross does not seem correct to me, it was the anguish that He wished to be free from.

Jesus' physical body was having a hard time handling this deep, deep woe. Jesus knew his body would be destroyed, but this burden of misery and anguish was huge! This burden of iniquity was so great that it caused His body to hemorrhage blood. Luke 22:44 says:

And being in an agony He prayed more earnestly: and His sweat was as it were great drops of blood falling down to the ground.

So Jesus did what every Christian should do, He prayed. And what was the answer to His prayer? Luke 22: 41-43 says:

And He was withdrawn from them about a stone's cast, and kneeled down, and prayed, saying, "Father, if Thou be willing, remove this cup from Me: nevertheless not My will,

---

[21] James and John

but Your will be done."

And there appeared an angel unto Him from heaven, strengthening Him.

This huge amount of mental anguish was not because He was "afraid" of the cross. The cross is the whole reason He was born. According to the Bible, He was slain before the foundation of the world.[22] The misery, the anguish, the bruising of the soul, the bruising of the psyche was nearly more than His earthly physical body could bear. His body was beginning to hemorrhage blood. So He prayed and the Father answered His prayer, He strengthened Him using ministering angels.

Jesus was bruised for our iniquity. Jesus took on this huge internal burden, this huge misery of the soul so that we might be free from any and all iniquity. Jesus took on this internal bruising to free our minds; he freed our psyches. He freed our souls.

How to Be Free

Freedom from iniquity or any other type of mental or emotional problem comes quite simply by giving it to God. People feel very comfortable asking God to forgive them of their sins, but they never seem to take the next step and ask to be free from the desire for that sin. Some feel comfortable asking for physical healing but not so comfortable for healing of the mind. So many people feel that it is their own personal responsibility to keep their mind right and whole. God can help you here! Ask God to remove the desires!

Choose. Remember, we always have a choice. Once you or the person you are praying for finally makes that decision to be truly free from the smoking, drinking, cursing, or some other desires, God can remove it. But do not think that we can trick God. He knows our hearts, He knows when we are truly being sincere. He knows when we truly want to be free from that thing.

Once we are truly sincere, then all we have to do is ask. We just have to pray in faith for God to remove that desire. We just have

---

[22] John 17:24, Hebrews 9:26, 1st Peter 1:20, Revelation 13:8

to pray in faith for God to change our nature in that area. He will do it.[23]

Even if we are predisposed to this desire because of a generational curse, we can be free of the desire. We may come from a long line of thieves, alcoholics, or gluttons. Are we sick and tired of it? We can be free from this curse. We can ask Jesus to come into our hearts and free us from this generational curse. He will do it. He has promised it. He will give us a new nature that is free from all of it.

---

[23] The way to pray for freedom from iniquity is the same way you pray for freedom from sickness. In one you are praying for physical bodily healing, in the other you are praying for healing of the soul.

Chapter 5

Paul's Thorn in the Flesh

That morning I woke with my eyes sealed shut again. The gunk that had poured out through the night formed dried-up crusts over my eyes and down into my hair. Laying in bed, I blindly fumbled for the alarm clock knocking it off the night-stand before I could finally shut it off. I tried to claw away the crusts so that I could open my eyes and see, but the yellow film was too thick this time. The top of my face felt like dry parched earth in the Arizona desert, crazed and cracked. Pawing the walls, I stumbled to the bathroom, smashed into the counter and began flushing and scrubbing my face in the sink.

It had been getting worse for weeks. I don't know why I put up with it. I always intended to pray my way through but just never seemed to have enough time to put forth a good honest effort. I didn't think a 5 second prayer was going to do it this time, so I kept putting it off until I had a good solid block of time to pray. And it was one of those busy times –working seven days a week, twelve hours a day, night school, the washer broke, the lawn mower broke, you know those times.

Several times a day I had to visit the sink to scrub and wipe the yellow ooze away. Periodically I would see chunks floating on the surface of my eyes, blocking my vision, it flowed constantly day and night. I was having trouble seeing.

Waking up like that was the last straw –I was going to get rid of this once and for all. By this time I had been healed by the power of God more times than I could count but this time I began to pray differently. I don't know why, but an odd thought had entered into my head. The eye infection reminded me of Paul's thorn. So many times people have stopped me from praying for them with that horrible statement that always goes something like, "Well you know God didn't heal Paul, maybe He won't heal me."

71

I do not know why people hold on to this. Maybe it is an escape hatch. Maybe this allows them to move on with their lives without asking any serious questions about why they didn't get the results they were expecting. People want to get healed but maybe they do not want to analyze themselves when they don't receive. Maybe they don't want to work too hard or pray too long. Maybe they need a way out. Maybe they need an excuse; they need a crutch. If they do not get healed maybe they will have to start asking some painful questions that they do not want to explore. I do not exactly know why they have this line of thinking but I had to put this question away once and for all so this time I prayed different.

I prayed, "Lord, if Paul's thorn in the flesh was a sickness that You *refused* to heal, then not only do I want You to not heal me, but make my eyes worse. If it was something other than that then please heal my eyes, Lord."

I had to have reassurance. I had to know without a shadow of doubt. I had to have the truth, not by being mentally convinced, but direct from God. There are too many people with degrees from various Bible colleges who have conflicting interpretations of the scriptures. Some even say that certain portions of the Bible are not inspired. I was tired of listening to all the different opinions. I was tired of listening to man's ideas of what happened and man's ideas of how God felt about it. I went to the source; I went to God. Let's see what God says about it.

Some people think that kind of a prayer is dangerous but I did it anyway. I was being reckless but I had to know the truth.

After I prayed, I leaned completely on the promises of the Word of God in the Bible, the promises that said that I would be healed. I believed fully that I was healed. The only way that healing works is through faith. You cannot pray, asking God to heal you, and then stare straight in the face of your symptoms wondering whether or not He is going to come through on His promises. You can't stare at your symptoms hoping they will change when you don't really believe.

I prayed for this healing the same that I would pray for any other. Stand on the Word, get my mind out of the way, believe and receive. I pulled my mind out of the way to let my faith rise up. I stopped focusing on my symptoms and focused on the promises found in the Word.

72

Just as I prayed, the Lord spoke to me and I *was* healed. Every bit of that yellow ooze disappeared that very day. I had that infection for over three weeks and it had been getting worse by the day. Now, it was completely and totally gone.

This time was no different than any other, the devil tried to attack and bring the sickness back. The devil tried to get me to doubt God's Word. After two weeks of being free of the symptoms, I woke up one morning and it was back. I knew it immediately because it itches. I couldn't stop thinking about it because I constantly wanted to scratch. The devil tries to bring a symptom back to make us doubt God's Word so that once we lose faith, it opens the door for the full return of the sickness.

Later that afternoon I got upset; I got angry at Satan. I got mad at the devil for challenging me and calling my God a liar. I yelled out at the top of my lungs. I screamed until my voice was gone and all that was left was a squeak. I rebuked it in the name of Jesus. I screamed out about forty times. My throat was scratchy from the screaming.

I bent over with my hands on my knees trying to catch my wind. It was cold out. I could see the steam of my breath as I gasped for air. It was a sweet release. No matter the symptoms, no matter the condition, I knew I was healed. I felt lighter; the demons had gone. I was free of them.

The symptoms stayed for the rest of the day, but I knew that condition would have no choice but to leave. The next morning I woke up and it was completely gone. It never returned.

Then I knew.

The Doctrine of Paul's Thorn in the Flesh

In chapter two we laid out an example proof that we might use to mentally convince people that prayer works and that God will heal them. Then we went on to give a brief explanation of how faith is developed. In chapter three we provided a framework of how to pray and in chapter four we showed that generational curses can be one of the sources of people's problems and additionally we showed that people can be healed not only physically but also spiritually and mentally.

So far I have been attempting to emphasize that praying for people is about so much more than the actual prayer itself. Much of the real work happens before we begin to pray as we really need to ensure that there is faith for the healing before we begin to pray. If the person simply does not believe then even if they are healed (through the strength of our own faith) they will probably quickly become sick again once they leave us.

So then in addition to the short proof provided in chapter one that you might use to help convince people and help them to believe, we will now show one of the common arguments against divine healing in this chapter and then we will show how to defeat this argument using the Bible. There are innumerable such arguments and we really need to learn to deal with as many of them as possible because we will need to get past these mental roadblocks before we even begin to pray.

So then let's talk about this argument. It is one of the most common reasons often heard for not being healed and I call it "Paul's thorn in the flesh." People say, "Well you know Paul was sick and God didn't heal him. Remember Paul's thorn in the flesh!" Then they smile knowingly and nod their heads as if they are part of some exclusive club.

In this work you will come across many different arguments such as this one on why divine healing does not, will not, or might not happen. Some of these arguments quote Bible verses. Paul's thorn in the flesh is only one such argument.

This chapter argues against Paul's thorn in the flesh but there are many other arguments that we will face and must learn to overcome. This chapter will briefly analyze this argument to see how the scriptures have been twisted then we will clearly show why this argument is false.

As the reasoning goes, Paul had a "thorn in the flesh" and God did not remove that "thorn" when Paul prayed. Let's first analyze this line of reasoning to understand the position. 2nd Corinthians 12:7-8 describes Paul's condition. Paul says:

> And lest I should be exalted above measure through the abundance of the revelations, a thorn in the flesh was given to me, a messenger of Satan to buffet me, lest I should be exalted above measure. For this thing I sought the Lord three times, that it might depart from me. (NKJV)

Here is another translation of that same passage:

> To keep me from becoming conceited because of these surpassingly great revelations, there was given me a thorn in my flesh, a messenger of Satan, to torment me. Three times I pleaded with the Lord to take it away from me. (NIV)

So many people know so little about the Bible, yet they seem to "know" that God did not answer Paul's prayer. People like to use Paul's thorn as an excuse for not receiving healing.

Well, I prayed and I didn't get healed, I guess I'm just like Paul, they think. Do not let that thought enter your head. That is a lie of the devil.

The standard interpretation is that Paul's thorn was an infection in his eyes. In Paul's writings, he dictated to a scribe, but Paul always wrote a few lines (usually the last few lines) of the letter so that people would know that it was an authentic letter from Paul. For example, in Thessalonians 3:17-18, the last few lines of the epistle, Paul writes:

> The salutation of Paul with mine own hand, which is the token in every epistle: so I write.
> The grace of our Lord Jesus Christ be with you all.

The last few lines of the letter to the Galatians are also written with Paul's own hand and there he says his writing was large. In Galatians 6:11, He says:

> You see how large a letter I have written unto you with mine own hand. (KJV)

Here is another translation of that same passage:

> See what large letters I use as I write to you with my own hand. (NIV)

We do not know if he meant that his letter was too long as in the King James' translation, or that his characters were bigger than normal as the New International Version says. No one knows because the original hand-written epistles are gone, we only have copies, so we cannot look at the actual characters to see if they were bigger than normal but some of the scholars say that he meant that his characters were very big. They argue that this is because his eyesight was so bad. They use Galatians 4:13-15 to justify this, Paul writes:

> You know how through infirmity of the flesh I preached

the gospel unto you at the first.[24]

And my temptation which was in my flesh you despised not, nor rejected; but received me as an angel of God, even as Christ Jesus.

Where is then the blessedness you spoke of? For I bear you record, that, if it had been possible, you would have plucked out your own eyes, and have given them to me.

And how did his eyesight become poor? He was exposed to a blinding light from God, which he never really recovered from, according to some of these same scholars.[25] This is the same light of God that came to Paul as he traveled on the road. This light identified itself as Jesus.

So in effect the "Paul's thorn in the flesh" doctrine actually says that Jesus caused Paul to be sick and then refused to heal him. It says that Jehovah God intentionally blinded Paul and then refused to heal him when he asked three times.

This line of thinking does not line up with scripture at all. Let's look at a few reasons why it is false.

The Thorn

No place in the Bible is the term *thorn* used to depict sickness. Numbers 33:55 says:

But if you will not drive out the inhabitants of the land from before you; then it shall come to pass, that those which you let remain shall be pricks in your eyes, and thorns in your sides, and shall vex you in the land where you dwell.

And Joshua 23:13 says:

Know for a certainty that the Lord your God will no more drive out any of these nations from before you; but they shall be snares and traps unto you, and scourges in your sides, and thorns in your eyes, until you perish from off this

---

[24] Paul may have preached while being sick "at the first" but he certainly never complained of any sickness later on. Galatians was Paul's first letter being written in AD 48 and it appears here that he is no longer sick for he uses the past tense. In none of the later letters does he describe himself as still having some sort of uncured eye condition.

[25] Acts 26:13

good land which the Lord your God hath given you.

So we see that the term *thorn* as it is used in the Bible is a person or a group of people that antagonize. The thorn in Biblical language is a person not a disease.

The Messenger
Next let's look at the next line in Paul's description:
There was given to me a thorn in the flesh, the messenger of Satan to buffet me

Paul says that it was a "messenger of Satan." The Greek word for *messenger* used here is actually the word αγγελος (Angelos) which can be translated both as *messenger* and *angel* and refers both to heavenly messengers (angelic beings) and earthly messengers (prophets.) The Hebrew word for *angel* is מלאד (malak), and also means *messenger*.[26] The prophet Malachi took his name from this word (basically calling himself "the messenger" or "the angel"). Sometimes *angel* can also be used to mean God –as in "the angel of the Lord" sometimes referring to the Holy Spirit.[27]

In the case of Paul's description of his thorn in the flesh, if we make a more direct translation we would say an *angel of Satan*. A "messenger" (angelos) could be an angelic/demonic being or a person, but it is certainly not a disease. This messenger is clearly either a human being or a demon.

The Buffeting
Again, here is Paul's description:
There was given to me a thorn in the flesh, the messenger of Satan to buffet me

Finally we see that this messenger, who was antagonizing Paul, was buffeting him. To buffet is to hit repeatedly. Why would

---

[26] Additionally, angelos and malak are also sometimes translated as ambassador. The typical meaning of angelos is a deputy, representative, envoy, or one who is sent from God (or Satan in this case).

[27] Acts 8:26

Paul say, "I am being repeatedly hit by this 'demon,'" instead of just saying, "I got hurt eyes?"

Now remember, Paul is one of the most open, clear and plain writing of all the prophets, yet people think what he says here is written in some kind of a code? In fact, the majority of Paul's writings were responses to questions from the churches. Paul was turned to as an authority who would clear up misunderstandings. They sent him their questions.

What Paul *clearly* says is that he is being antagonized repeatedly by a messenger of Satan. In 1st Corinthians 4:11-13, Paul lists the buffetings by Satan that he has been suffering from. He says:

> Even unto this present hour we both hunger, and thirst, and are naked, and are buffeted, and have no certain dwelling place;
>
> And labor, working with our own hands: being reviled... being persecuted...being defamed...we are made as the filth of the world, and are the off scouring of all things unto this day.

So here is a list of Paul's buffetings and sickness is not on the list. It is not listed because Paul's "thorn in the flesh" had nothing to do with illness.[28]

So many people mention Paul's thorn and say, "Oh, sometimes God says, 'No' when a person prays to be healed, that's why I'm not healed."

That is completely false. God never says, "No" to healing.[29] It is amazing to me that people can deny the simple and direct Word of God found throughout the entire Bible that says God heals and then point at this *one scripture* that really says nothing about sickness, and twist it. If you did not receive your healing then there may be some other reason, but it is not God saying, "No." God heals!

---

[28] 1st and 2nd Corinthians were both written around AD 56, probably from Philippi or Ephesus (see Acts 20:1-6) before Paul's first imprisonment in Rome in AD 60. Paul later wrote Ephesians, Philippians, Colossians, Philemon, 1st and 2nd Timothy, and Titus. He does not mention any continuing or past eye problem, nor does he complain of any sickness in any of these letters.

[29] The reason why some requests for healing do not come immediately will become clear later. It has more to do with spiritual strongholds that need to be fixed first.

Now, this is not being pointed out to try and put people down who did not receive a healing. I want people to be healed and will do anything I can to help achieve this goal. It is only the devil who is putting some kind of a block in front of the healing. This is the one we need to be angry with. The fact of the matter is that God heals and that God does not say, "*No!*" to healing. God wants to heal us!

Hopefully this chapter has shed some light on one of the many arguments out there that people use against divine healing. Beginning in section three, we are going to look much deeper at some of this introductory material and in the process begin to more clearly see some of the reasons that people have not received healing after being prayed for and show how we, as prayer warriors, can change in order to become more successful and see God's work be done in more people's lives.

Section 3: Becoming a Prayer Warrior

Chapter 6

Responsibility

Walking through the furniture store, I was praying in an almost inaudible voice whispering godly praises that people around me could not hear. I pushed two of my three young children in a double stroller and the four year-old walked next to me. I felt the anointing swirling around me as I glided between sofas and dining room sets on display. I was feeling a little intoxicated in my own little moveable bubble of spiritual atmosphere.

I was a bit giddy. I had recently been reading a Smith Wigglesworth book in which he said he tried to be full of the anointing all the time. No matter where he was, he prayed to be anointed. This was new to me; I mean I spoke to God all the time but it seemed like I seldom sensed the presence of God except sometimes when I was in my private prayer place or in church during service. I was giddy like a grammar-school girl who just got her hair done in those big, bouncy, Shirley Temple curls. I was actually out in public, doing normal everyday things and the anointing of the Holy Spirit was swirling around me. This was cool!

As we headed for the exit, the sliding glass doors automatically popped open and my oldest son flashed out of the store into the parking lot. He was running as fast as his four-year-old legs could carry him.

He giggled, "Race me to the car, Daddy!"

It was something I had taught him without weighing the full consequences. We competed in everything. We were always racing each other here or there. We would run together all the time. I almost always let him win.[30]

It happened so fast. I couldn't get from behind the stroller quick enough to stop him. Just then a teenager driving a full-size

---

[30] I don't have to let him win anymore. He is grown now and beats me easily.

83

truck roared into the roadway in front of the store. He was going to mow down my son!

Time instantly slowed. I saw every detail of the driver's face. Sounds were muffled to my ears as if I was too far away. I felt like I was viewing the scene through binoculars, just a spectator. My feet were glued as if the pavement was covered in molasses. I felt like I was running in place. The ground moved below me like I was on the wrong direction on an airport people-mover.

The whole story of our life together flashed before my eyes. I saw my own childhood, my adolescence, everything. I saw my son's birth on that cold dark night. I remembered how he looked coming down that hallway as the nurse carried him into the room for the first time. I remembered how sweetly my wife held him the morning after all that pain. I remembered our laughter at his innocent sweetness. I remembered laying awake at night, next to him, listening to him breathe. I remembered the first time that I cried from happiness. It was like I had the eyes of a fly with a thousand lenses; each lens contained a different image, a different part of me, and a different part of my life with him.

The sound of the roaring truck could not enter my ears. I couldn't hear anything. I was surrounded by a muffled silence. The red on the truck was so bright![31] I could see every detail of expression on the driver's face. He was so totally engrossed in the country music that was blaring from his stereo. One bent arm hung low out of the driver's side window so he could hand tap the beat of the song out on his door while his other hand gripped the peak of the steering wheel forming a forward pointing fist. An old, torn, green John Deere hat was bent tight, curling across his forehead letting light brown, greasy straight hair peek out and partially cover his ears.

As the red truck sped by in slow motion, missing my son by some few inches, time was bending all around me and my brain was

---

[31] This time-bending phenomenon that I was experiencing is called Tachypsychia by Psychologists. It is a response of the brain brought on by stress. As the brain is flooded by excess neurotransmitters, time perceived lengthens, making events appear to slow down and the person experiencing it sometimes has transient partial color blindness and tunnel vision.

completely turned off. My brain was flooded with input. My head was in autopilot. I couldn't think. [32]

Instantaneously full of rage, I swaggered boldly out of the store and spat out a Holy Spirit filled curse upon that young driver. I didn't use profanity; I actually cursed him spiritually. God did not tell me to do this. I was not Peter dealing with Ananias and Sapphira.[33] I wasn't trained for this. I wasn't thinking. It was the old, carnal human inside of me erupting like a crusty, decaying volcano lying dormant for eons then one day wiping out a village. I was misusing the power of God. Something foul inside of me woke up ready to spout stench. This was all me, yet it was anointed. I felt the Spirit of God going forth on my breath, flying toward the vehicle.

Oh no! What have I done?

My mind suddenly woke up but it was too late to stop it. The Word had been spoken, the Word was going forth. It was too late to grab the words out of the air. They were already spoken, already moving, traveling like a just-fired arrow, violently seeking, pushing the air out of its way as it seeks its target.

Just at that moment something happened.

Just at the moment of the last word exiting my mouth, something happened.

Just at the moment of the last syllable of the last word exiting my mouth, something happened.

---

[32] Tachypsychia happens because our brains are actually trying to help us during life threatening situations by boosting our perception of both the external and internal. Time becomes elastic and the texture of the world floods into your senses. I perceived everything at its highest resolution. On the surface this seems like a great feature of the human brain, but there is a downside. In these extreme situations where the brain enters this "flight or fight" mode, cognitive ability drops dramatically. We perceive everything around us in extreme detail, but we cannot seem to think straight, we cannot make a correct decision or even make a decision at all. This is why training is emphasized so much in stressful jobs. Soldiers, police officers, and firemen are trained so vigorously that their responses become almost automatic in extreme situations. They might not be able to think things through so they rely on their training.

[33] See the 5th Chapter of Acts.

The truck was moving quickly and was already about one hundred meters away when another young boy about the same age as my son ran out into the parking lot. This boy was a little faster than my son, he was directly in the path of the roaring truck when he stopped and looked up at it. The hair on the back of my neck stood up.

What have I done?

My mind spun like a Kansas tornado into a flurry of intense self-condemnation, *I have become death. I am the bringer of death. I am the minister of death. I am the destroyer of worlds. I am the destroyer of lives. I am the destroyer of families.*

The spirit had gone forth, the air was not in my lungs. My breath was gone. I stood there motionless. Paralyzed. Parents and onlookers screamed in horror. There was nothing they could do. Their feet were glued just like mine were some moments earlier.

The brakes screeched like nails on a chalkboard.

Crash!!!!

The truck swerved to avoid the unmoving child and smashed into the concrete barrier separating the parked cars from the lane. Sparks flew from underneath the truck as the metal made a scraping sound. By the mercy of God no one was injured and only damage was done to the vehicle.

As I watched this all unfold in the distance, a deep woe quickly shadowed my spirit. It took my breath away. I felt a darkness in the sky over me as a cloud quickly blotted out the sun. I knew that I had misused the power of God. I knew that I had used the anointing in carnality.

Others probably thought little of what just happened and quickly forgot about it. *Nothing really happened did it? No one was hurt, right?*

But for me, this memory is so burned into my spirit that it is something that will always be with me. I will never forget.

Progression of Increase

In our first section, we provided examples of some of the problems that people can run into when praying for others. Continuing into the second section, we laid out a proof that you might use to mentally convince people that prayer works and then we briefly explained how faith is developed. We also provided a framework of how to pray and showed that one of the sources of people's problems can be generational curses. Additionally, we showed that people can be healed not only physically but also spiritually and mentally. Finally, the second section showed one of the arguments against divine healing and provided a short proof against it in order to provide one example of some of the arguments that prayer warriors will come against.

As we begin our third and final section, we are going to shift the focus of our camera away from the actual act of praying for people and turn our lens onto ourselves to look at ways that we can improve, before, during and after the prayer, in order to greatly improve our success. Later in the third section, in the power, faith is substance, and authority chapters, we will revisit, amplify and explain introductory material that was presented in section two.

So now let's begin to look at ourselves and how God will change us as we begin to accept that He has called us to pray for others.

Once we fully accept that we are who God says that we are, people who can and should pray for each other and expect results, we will see a tremendous increase in power and authority in the area that God called us. The quickening power of the Holy Spirit will water the seed inside of us. God will never force anything on us, but once we accept it and start walking in it, then God will quicken it and it will become spiritually alive.

The more that we pray for people, the more that we will learn and the more spiritually mature we will become. Like natural life, there is a progression of things. You would not give your car keys to a baby or even a ten-year old. Even a young man with a new driver's license might have the car only with limitations. Likewise, God tries us and matures us. As we become more responsible and trustworthy God gives us more authority and power.

God could have prevented me from cursing that young driver in the previous story, but He allowed me so that I would mature. I had only a small portion of His trust and His authority over His power at that time. Now I have matured and have more. I can tell you without question that I will never misuse the power of God in that way ever again and God knows that. He now trusts me with more. Let's

87

look at a Biblical example of a Prophet misusing God's power. 2nd Kings 2:23 and 24 says:

> And he [Elisha] went up from there unto Beth-el: and as he was going up by the way, there came little children out of the city, and mocked him, and said unto him, "Go up, you bald head; go up, you bald head."
>
> And he turned back, and looked on them, and cursed them in the name of the Lord. And there came forth two she-bears out of the wood and mauled forty-two children.

The Bible is full of examples of great men and women of God who made mistakes and we should learn from them. Elisha was wrong in cursing these children. God did not tell him to maul and maim forty-two little children. They were little children! He cursed them for his own fleshly reasons.

Notice also that Elisha was very new to his calling as he just received it a few verses earlier.[34] He was an old, bald-headed man but young in the Lord. He was spiritually immature and he made a mistake. Every servant of God has to traverse these early days and many will make mistakes. Yet even risking making a mistake we all want more of God's supernatural power in our lives.

Almost every servant of God *wants* to walk in more power and more authority. Almost every minister wants to serve God more fully. People cry out to God all the time, "Send us your rain, send us your anointing, and send us your power." The whole world groans for a deeper manifestation of the spiritual and God's healing touch. Yet so many go on with weak ministries, some even powerless. Why?

One of the several reasons is a lack of trustworthiness. Can God trust us to **not** use His great and mighty power for carnality?

This is a hard question and if we stopped here then this would be a terrible writing. But we do not stop. Next we will see how to progressively squeeze out the carnal desires and walk more worthy of God's power. This is one of the wonderful keys to a greater manifestation of the power of God in our prayers.

---

[34] Some argue that there could have been a great span of time in-between these few verse, but in any case he showed great spiritual immaturity.

Temptation, Desire, Sin, and Death

James 1:14-15 says:

> But every man is tempted, when he is drawn away of his own lust, and enticed. Then when nature has conceived, it brings forth sin: and sin, when it is finished, brings forth death. (NKJV)

Here is another translation of that same passage:

> But each one is tempted when, by his own evil desire, he is dragged away and enticed. Then, after desire has conceived, it gives birth to sin; and sin, when it is full-grown, gives birth to death. (NIV)

There are four intimately linked steps here: temptation, desire, sin, and death. If we are to walk in real power, the holy power of God, then we must be trustworthy. To be trustworthy, we must not only *not sin*, but also *not desire*.

Remember our earlier chapter on iniquity. Remember what was said, God can remove the desire, but that doesn't mean He will remove the temptation. In fact, it will always be present. God is not going to remove the sexy billboards and cover up the scantily clad women so that we do not sin. God is not going to instantly eliminate addictive drugs from the planet so that we do not sin. God is not going to stop people from cutting us off in traffic so that we do not sin. God will not remove the temptation. God is not going to stop the children from calling us "bald-head" or the teenager from almost plowing down our children in their red trucks so that we do not sin. But God can remove the desire to sin if we let Him and ask Him.

Notice the pattern: temptation, desire, sin, and death. In the case of the story at the beginning of the chapter, I was *trying* to walk holy. I was suppressing any desire to sin, yet the desire was still present somewhere deep inside of me. This suppression of our inner nature works in day-to-day living but what about when extraordinary temptation comes? When that truck passed inches from my child's body it was too much temptation for me to hold back. I lost control of the desire to lash out. Desire conceived sin and gave birth to death.

Notice that in some translations of our verse in *James* the word *desire* is translated as *nature*. It is the very nature of the person that is at fault and has to be changed. This is not something that we can do! We cannot go merrily along, looking good on the outside while we have hidden desires that are part of our very nature and expect to be blessed with great godly power. If we are to pray with great authority with signs and wonders then our very **nature** must be changed.

The process of this *change of nature* is really the same as already laid out in previous chapters so it will not be repeated, but the purpose of this chapter is to open our eyes to this hidden armada of death that may be lurking deep inside of us. Once identified, it is only a matter of prayer and perhaps some fasting to be free from it.

Remember, temptation will always be there, enticing us, trying to lead us astray. No matter how much we pray, temptation will be ever present. It will never leave. But it is the desire we need to remove. When the nature has conceived then sin gives birth to death. We do not want to be ministers of death! The temptation will never go away but if we are to walk worthy of God's power we must remove the desire. Without the inner desire, we will not be able to be enticed by temptation into bringing forth death.

The Apostles' Pride

Now I would like to focus on one specific area of desire. It is one of the largest stumbling blocks for God's people and is pride and selfishness.

When God starts progressively using us more and we begin to see our prayers answered, pride can rear its ugly head. It is so hard. In trying to give witness and tell people of God's wonderful works, we can here people say, "I did this... I laid my hands on him and..."

Be careful to keep *self* in its place. Yes we did the work, but only what our Father in heaven showed us and God performed the miracle. We are only vessels of God's anointing.

Now we are going to look at a dramatic example of the Apostle's pride and how it leads them down the path to become ministers of death. It is a bit longer example but I like it because it shows a progression of thought in the Apostles and how that temptation and desire gave birth to sin and death. Luke 9 starts:

> Then He [Jesus] called His twelve disciples together, and gave them power and authority over all devils, and to cure diseases. And He sent them to preach the kingdom of God, and to heal the sick.

10 And the Apostles, when they returned, told Him all that they had done.

Clearly the Apostles were walking in power and authority. Jesus anointed them and the Holy Spirit was with them to perform mighty signs and wonders. Yet when they returned they did not give glory to God but told "all that *they* had done."

Of course, this phrase "all that they had done" could be read several different ways but still a question begins to form in my mind. Why were they not praising God and giving God glory for what God had done *through* them?

Shortly after the Apostles return from performing many miracles Jesus tests their faith. Jesus asks the Apostles to feed the multitudes. They were walking in signs and wonders already, now Jesus tests them to see where their faith stops. Luke 9:13 continues:

But He said unto them, "You give them to eat." And they said, "We have no more but five loaves and two fishes; except we should go and buy meat for all this people."

So we see that Jesus asks *them* to feed the multitudes. Of course they were too spiritually immature at this point to do what Jesus did, multiply the fish and loaves, and this is what Jesus is trying to point out to them. At this moment, Jesus was starting to see something in the Apostles that needed correction and instruction. He was showing them that it was not about self or pride, it was about God. Luke 9:23 and 24 goes on:

And He said to them all, "If any man will come after Me, let him deny himself, and take up his cross daily, and follow Me. For whosoever will save his life shall lose it: but whosoever will lose his life for My sake, the same shall save it."

Jesus was trying to guide them. *Apostles, please stop looking to yourself. Deny yourself. Deny self. It is not about you. It is about the power of God that is in you.* Still the Apostles failed to recognize the significance of Jesus words. Luke 9:46-48 continues:

Then there arose a reasoning among them, which of them should be greatest.

And Jesus, perceiving the thought of their heart, took a child, and set him by Him, and said unto them, "Whosoever shall receive this child in my name receives Me. and whosoever shall receive Me receives Him that sent Me: for he that is least among you all, the same shall be great."

Over and over in this chapter we see Jesus warning them to deny *self.* We see the warning like a bright flashing red light and clanging alarm bell at the coming of a train crossing. Deny self. None are to be great except God. Glorify God not self. Let loose of pride. With the nature of pride you are only headed to destruction and death. Yet they did not hear and the pride continued. The lifting up of one's self in the Apostles did not stop. Continuing in Luke 9:49-50 we read:

And John answered and said, "Master, we saw one casting out devils in Your name; and we forbad him, because he followed not with us."

And Jesus said unto him, "Forbid him not: for he that is not against us is for us."

In effect John is pointing his finger out to others who are not Apostles and saying, "You are not the chosen! You are not with us! You have not been walking with Jesus as we have! We are the chosen, not you!"

Pride and self is creeping out and beginning to show itself outwardly in their behavior. The question to Jesus seemed innocent, yet it revealed so much. The Apostles have not yet let go of that nature of pride and self seated deep inside of them. So far the results have only been innocent because there has not yet been a great temptation. Remember, "Every man is tempted...then when nature has conceived, it brings forth sin: and sin, when it is finished, brings forth death." Now see what happens in the face of greater temptation. Luke 9:52-54 continues:

[Jesus] sent messengers before His face: and they went and entered into a village of the Samaritans to make ready for Him.

And they [the Samaritans] did not receive Him, because His face was as though He would go to Jerusalem.

And when His disciples, James and John saw this, they said, "Lord, can we command fire to come down from heaven, and consume them, even as Elijah did?"

These Apostles were ready to destroy the Samaritans. They were ready to use anointed Holy Ghost power for their own carnal nature and desires. Their hearts were full of pride and self and had absolutely no problem condemning these unknowing souls to death. Listen to Jesus' words:

But He [Jesus] turned, and rebuked them, and said, "You know not what manner of spirit you are of.

For the Son of man is not come to destroy men's lives, but to save them." And they went to another village.

The Apostles had desires and nature that were prideful, selfish, and sinful and if left unchecked this nature would conceive sin and give birth to death. If we are to walk in true Holy Ghost power and the will of the Lord, we must eradicate this desire, this pride, this *self*.

Temptation will never go away. There will always be people trying to stop us or prevent us from going forward but if there is no desire, there will be no sin. If we can change our very internal nature, then there is nothing inside to conceive sin no matter what the temptation. Cut it off at the root.

We may have occasional successes or see some divine healing, but without the removal of these types of internal desires God will never trust us with great supernatural power.

Self Righteousness

The errors of pride and self we have previously discussed are directly related to self-righteousness so let's discuss that briefly also. We have to remember that we are not righteous of ourselves, we are only righteous in that we have put on Jesus. No matter how many good works we do we are only righteous in that we have put on Jesus. No matter how many people are healed when we pray we are only righteous in that we have put on Jesus. When the Judge looks down from heaven He judges us righteous because He sees the blood of the Lamb, not our sin.

Always remember that no matter the condition of a person, we are all equally lost except for the blood of Jesus. Always remember that no matter the condition of a person, we are all equally unworthy except for the blood of Jesus. Romans 3:12 says:

There is none who does good, no, not one.

So as we look at pride and self-righteousness, let's look deeper into the way we feel about others. If we despise others or look down on others then we are still guilty of a form of pride and self-righteousness and we can be disqualified. Here is an example. In Luke 18:9-14, Jesus gives one of the most well-known of parables concerning self-righteousness:

And he spoke this parable unto certain which trusted in themselves that they were righteous [self righteous], and despised others:

"Two men went up into the temple to pray; the one a Pharisee, [Priest or Pastor] and the other a publican [common man].

The Pharisee stood and prayed thus with himself, 'God, I thank you, that I am not as other men are, extortioners, unjust, adulterers, or even as this publican.

I fast twice in the week, I give tithes of all that I possess.'

And the publican, standing afar off, would not lift up so much as his eyes unto heaven, but smote upon his breast, saying, 'God be merciful to me a sinner.'

I tell you, this man [the common man] went down to his house justified rather than the other [the Pharisee]: for every one that exalts himself shall be abased; and he that humbles himself shall be exalted."

This is a well-known story that is often taught so we will only draw out a few less emphasized points.

First notice that Jesus was describing those who were self-righteous and "despised others." There is a strong link between these two. Not many Christians would admit that they are self-righteous, but ask another question. Do we despise others? Is there anyone that we despise? Is there a person we avoid because we just do not like them?

Jesus linked these two characteristics together because they have the same root. If we have one, we have the other. If we despise others, then we are self-righteous. If we are self-righteous then we will not walk fully in power because we cannot be fully trusted.

Remember, "There is none who does good, no, not one." No matter how much we have done for the kingdom of God, our righteousness is not caused by our actions. Our righteousness is through the blood, just like everyone else on the planet. We might lay hands on the sick and they recover, yet we have no room to boast. We are only righteous because of God's mercy on us.

The second point to pull out from this parable is that the Pharisee was probably telling the truth in his prayer. He *was* a righteous man by man's standards. Look at all the things he did for God and God's kingdom. He was probably highly regarded in his community. This is a by-product of being a servant of God. We should never let that go to our head. We are no more worthy than the worst murderer on the earth who has given his life to Jesus. We are all servants of the most high; it is He who deserves ALL the glory.

Additionally, the publican was *not* a righteous man by man's standards. Look at all the things he did against God's kingdom. Yet it was the motive of the heart that God saw.

Examine Your Heart

These examples of selfishness and pride are only a few of the many things that can block our relationship with God and road block the amount of power He gives us. I only highlight these because they are probably two of the most common problems that Christians have.

So then, the purpose of this chapter is to make us aware of inner desires that may be lurking deep within us that may cause us to fall or block us from walking in true Holy Ghost power. It is these inner desires that may be blocking us from walking in greater anointing and greater power. So clearly then we must have our hearts examined to be rid of this mess.

I am sure that many of you have done this. I also continually tried to do this. Even before I laid that Holy Spirit filled curse on the teenager driving the red truck, I had been examining my heart. Yet there was something there that I didn't see. How is this possible?

So many people examine their hearts and perceive that it is fine. They see nothing that would lead them to fall. And the little things they do see they take care of right away. Yet there are things that are missed and that is the problem; we cannot truly and completely perceive our own hearts. Jeremiah asks this question in 17:9 he says:

The heart is deceitful above all things and desperately wicked; who can know it?

So many people think they can simply sit back and peer inside of themselves and know their own heart. Maybe we can look at our thoughts a bit or think about our past and remember how we have acted in certain situations, but there is only One who can truly know our heart and that is God. 1st Kings 8:39 shows us that God *alone* know the hearts of men. And in Revelation 2:23 God declares:

I am He who searches the hearts and minds.

We need the piercing eyes of God to examine our hearts and to expose our failings. We must step boldly to the throne of God and ask Him to show us our weaknesses. We must step forth with an open mind and an open heart asking God to expose it so that it can be cleaned, sanctified, and made holy. We cannot step forward, see it, and do nothing about it. We must step forward with the knowledge that when we see it, we will then ask for the carnal desires to be removed. We must step forward with the full knowledge and understanding that it may be painful.

We all want to see a greater manifestation of the power of God. We want to see God glorified. Yet to walk in this glory and power requires separation, sanctification, trustworthiness, and responsibility. Saints, let us let God examine our hearts so that the carnal desires lurking in the recesses might be exposed to light. Let Him open our eyes to our failings so that they may be swept clean and away. Let's walk worthy of the power that God has placed in us. Let's walk worthy and *be* the son or daughter of God that we are called to be.

Chapter 7

Operating in Love

Beads of hot, salty sweat dripped off my forehead and into my eyes as I focused on him. Wearing old wrinkled pajamas and bedroom slippers full of teeth marks from his loyal dog, he slouched into a couch that wrapped around him as if it was molded specifically for his body. I stared intently at his weathered face peering past his haggard chin that had not been shaved in several days, seeing an outer shell of worn-out flesh.

He was going to die soon. Cancer had all but taken his life. His body was weak and wasting away. He had lost so much weight and looked so skinny. Constantly tired and in pain, he stopped the chemotherapy treatments. It was God or nothing for him. He was making a stand.

He slept long but restless most of the days and when he wasn't sleeping he tried to pray. Unfortunately he couldn't pray much because he felt he had to give time to the stream of visitors. People from all over were constantly knocking at his door. They were trying to do the right thing, coming to say goodbye to a man that was about to die, coming to say goodbye to a man that had so affected the direction of their lives. They didn't realize how depressed that made him. In their eyes he was already dead.

He was in physical pain but he was all right with that. He wasn't sad to leave this world either. Outwardly he looked melancholy, like someone who was just waiting to go. He didn't say much, just sat there, sunken eyes deeply staring into the unknown. It was almost a look of daze.

As I peered inward I began to see something else. I didn't know him. He had only asked me to come pray for him, but I suddenly *saw* him. The Holy Spirit revealed the internals of his very heart and spirit to me. I didn't know him, but I saw that he had been a good husband and father, his wife would be taken care of and his children were fine, they were all grown up with their own jobs and lives anyway. It wasn't that he was worried about finances or worldly concerns, but there was something else. As I stared at him in the silence I felt like I was trying to look around a corner inside of him.

What was it? What was the dark secret lurking in the corner? What was hiding in there?[35]

An ordained minister of the gospel, this man had touched many lives. He had preached the gospel with fire. He did not head a church but he preached at times and his sermons were full of power and people remembered them.

As I looked at his eyes I remembered that this man was well known for his gaze. He had the type of light gray, subtly piercing eyes that saw through a man. Some people didn't like to talk to him directly because they felt like he was seeing into them, that somehow their secrets were exposed. This time it was me who was trying to see inside, trying to look at his heart. Staring hard, I looked inside of him, my unblinking eyes watered from the intensity.

Then suddenly it appeared. The illumination of God lit up and I saw it. I had a revelation of his problem, the problem that God wanted dealt with first. It was as if a flashlight all suddenly clicked on and the beam of light cast down onto his problem. I could see it so plain! This ordained minister, this fiery preacher, was unsure if he truly made heaven.

I would have never guessed. No one knew. None of the hundreds of people visiting him knew.

He was a minister of the gospel, of course he was saved! No one would suspect this!

I nervously spoke it out loud in a shaky voice that surprised me, "The Lord tells me that you read Hebrew 6:4-6 some time ago

---

[35] You might be thinking, "Well, why didn't you just pray for him to be healed?" But that is the whole problem. We have to pray how God leads us to pray. We have to see what is the most important thing to God. We have to see what God wants dealt with first. So many people have so many problems and many times the prayer warriors make the mistake of dealing with the most physically evident problem first or the one that the people ask for. The problem that the people ask relief from can be the last one God wants to take care of. First see what the most important thing is for God. First find out God's priority then take care of that first. What is more important, a man's soul or his body? What is more important, what God wants done or what we want done?

98

and now you think you are lost. The Lord showed me that you had sinned some time ago and now you think you are lost."[36]

His face burst forth in a shower of red. He squinted his eyes shut hard and tears leaked out. He slowly sobbed out loud.

Cautiously leaning closer to me, he grasped my shirtsleeve tightly, cutting off the flow of blood to my hand as his piercing eyes suddenly looked up and went right through me. He knew that there was no way I could have known that, even his wife did not know that.[37]

His harsh voice choked in desperation, "Help me, brother! I can't go out like this! I don't want to go to Hell!"

He truly believed that he was eternally condemned. He was looking for an out, maybe there was a misunderstanding, but in his mind he had fallen too far. He thought he could not be redeemed. He thought he was headed straight for Hell. He though he was lost![38]

He explained where he had fell. He told me all that he had done then waxed sullen and poetic as he slumped back into the couch that had held him for many years, "The sun rises and the sun sets. Days pass so fast in the life of a man. My life is as the blink of the eyelid of a fly to God. We are as nothing and He is everything."

He paused for a long while with his eyes closed, seemingly not breathing, then said with an air of utter finality, "Miserable is the life of a man who is separated from God and does not know it. And more miserable is the life of a man who is separated from God and does know."

An unbearably loud silence filled the room. My ears began to ring painfully. I didn't know what to say. How could I handle this? I felt like an idiot. What was I doing here? I mean I thought I was

---

[36] Hebrews 6:4-6 says: For it is impossible for those who were once enlightened, and have tasted the heavenly gift, and have become partakers of the Holy Spirit, and have tasted the good word of God and the powers of the age to come, if they fall away, to renew them again to repentance, since they crucify again for themselves the Son of God, and put Him to an open shame.

[37] He told me later that no one knew.

[38] Whether or not this man could actually lose his salvation is a completely different question. I cover that question in great detail in my first book *The Indwelling: An Introduction to a New Relationship with God.*

coming here to pray for his sickness for a little while and then going out to dinner with my wife.

Who did I think I was, coming to this man's home, this ordained minister's house to pray for him? I wasn't even ordained myself! I was a nobody.

I felt like crying. There was such a despair floating in the room. I felt like getting up and walking out. I needed some air! The pressure was so intense. Something was squeezing my head and my brains were about to pop out of the top of my head.

I closed my eyes and looked down. I obviously couldn't leave. No way. But what was I gong to say? He knew all the salvation scriptures better than I did. What could I tell him? Silently I prayed, "Lord, I can't handle this. I am so far out of my league. You are going to have to do this." I was so desperate. Next to me sat a man who was about to die and thought he was going to Hell and I had nothing for him. A thick, furry coat called worthless and weak was wrapped around me tight.

I began to pray and ask God to strengthen me. I remembered Jesus at the garden and how God sent Him angels to strengthen Him.

As I continued to pray I slowly began to feel stronger. The darkness in the room faded. Words began to pop into my head. I wasn't looking at him, I was staring at the brown wood paneling on his far wall, both of us in silence, when I heard myself almost unconsciously reciting the words out loud, "The work of a man's hands is as dust in the sands of time for who will remember him when he is gone? And the blood of a man's body? As dust. The life pumping through his heart? As dust."

I wondered where these words were coming from and where this was going, but not able to say or think anything on my own, I just let go and continued speaking, "Oh, that we would have awoke from the moment we were born to know the true reality of things. Instead we bumble about in this world like blind moles full of false priorities in a hidden daylight, feverishly storing food for winter, afraid that others will steal it, when the truest food is given away openly and freely and in sincerity."

I had no idea what God was doing. I felt like this was making it worse, yet I continued letting God feed me the words, "When a person loses something dear to him, he consoles himself with a multitude of other dear things; wife and children, money and things, or perhaps the notion that he is still healthy or still can accomplish

100

many things with the life he has left. But when a man has no comfort in his spirit, with what can he replace it? When a man has lost the most precious thing, the thing that his heart longs for with all his being, the thing that can never be replaced, he cannot be comforted. With what can he regain his hope? What power can provide more than a mere distraction from the tremblings of his heart?"

My voice, choking out the last words, revealed the intensity of suffering I felt in the deep waters of my heart.[39]

He sobbed slowly with his head down. It was the cry of a thirsty cub who waits anxiously, hiding in the tall reeds at the edge of the pond, knowing the water is so close but not able to taste its life giving water lest he be shredded by the hungry lions that drink there.

I began to tell him things almost spontaneously. It was like I was hearing it myself for the first time, "You know that all those letters Paul wrote in the Bible were written as responses to questions sent to him from the churches he started."

"I know that brother," He said despondently, not knowing where I was headed.

"Well, if Paul wrote in Hebrews 6 that people cannot be redeemed after falling away, don't you think that somewhere else in that same letter Paul would have explained what he meant by 'falling away?' "

He sat up straight. I got his attention and the Lord got mine. We began to look back through Hebrews, scanning every chapter and verse, trying to understand what exactly Paul meant when suddenly we both stopped at the 3rd chapter and 12th verse.[40] Suddenly he realized that he was not lost, he had not fallen away. Suddenly the cloud lifted.

See, it didn't matter that he fell. Just the fact that God was calling the man back to Him was a certain sign that he was not eternally lost. Why would God call a person back who could not come back? Sure he made mistakes, but we all do. Most of us are imperfect, I think. Most of us make little mistakes everyday.

---

[39] I did not understand the purpose of these words God gave me at the time, but I know now that it was a way of connecting with his spirit where it was and in the condition that it was in at that time.

[40] Hebrews 3:12 says: See to it, brothers, that none of you has a sinful, unbelieving heart that turns away from the living God

101

I asked, "Did you feel God calling you back from the edge of sin?"

"Yes, brother," He said with a broad grin, knowing the meaning of the question.

God forgave him. There is no sin that is too great that God won't forgive a repentant sinner. There is no gulf too wide that God cannot step over to reach us.

This scripture just came to me then, "I am convinced that neither death nor life, neither angels nor demons, neither the present nor the future, nor any powers, neither height nor depth, nor anything else in all creation, will be able to separate us from the love of God that is in Christ Jesus our Lord." [41]

Over the next hour I spent with him, he was gradually restored to the Lord. One by one we worked through every past offense and every mistake. We removed the barriers and bad teachings. His thoughts were his enemy, not his body. The cancer in his body was nothing compared to the price of his very soul.

Finally a joy swept through the room. I felt so strong in my spirit that the work was done. I felt a godly confirmation. We were finished, the Holy Spirit told me to do no more. I mean, I *wanted* to pray for his physical healing, but he did not ask and the Lord did not tell me to do it. The man could not stop smiling and hugging me. His body was still weak from the cancer, but he was exuberant. He was excited.

"I am saved!" He bellowed as loud as his cancer riddled body would allow. It was a fresh revelation. It was all new, all over again.

Over the next few weeks I heard reports from people who were saved when they went to visit this man. From his deathbed he was preaching to all who came to visit him. People left amazed. That same stream of visitors was still coming to pay their last respects. They came to say goodbye to him. They were simply fulfilling their duty to a pastor but they were shocked by what they saw. His joy and excitement was bubbling over. Here lay a man on his deathbed, body shriveled and in decay, preaching the fire of God with all that he had.

I again asked permission from the Lord to go to pray for his physical healing but the Lord did not release me, "This is a true war-

---

[41] Romans 8:38-39

rior for the kingdom, we need him on the battlefield," I pleaded but the Lord said, "I do not want you to go."

I couldn't understand it. Maybe the man needed to be convinced so that the Lord would release me. Maybe the Lord was sending someone else. I called the man on the phone. He thanked me for offering, paused for a pregnant second, then hoarsely said, "I love you brother."

I pressed him again, "Don't you want to be healed?"

Pausing for an hour-long second he repeated with a deep and craggy voice full of deep sincerity, "I love you brother."

I realized that he did not want it. I do not know why but perhaps he wanted to go home. Perhaps he was ready.

A few days later his heart stopped pumping blood and he died. He died at peace with a smile on his face and joy in his heart. He went to be with the Lord.

Steps

In our first few chapters, we listed "steps" in explaining how faith works and how to pray. This was done only to establish a simple framework. For the remainder of the book, we are going to briskly move away from that framework to teach more comprehensive principles. It is not that our framework was necessarily wrong, only that it was an oversimplification and then does not necessarily handle every situation. This particular chapter explains some of the downfalls of exclusively following step-by-step procedures and describes a better way to operate.

So why then are steps so popular if they don't work all the time?

Well, whenever someone asks you how to do something, what they are really asking for is a series of steps to accomplish the task. In effect they are asking for a set of rules, a step-by-step procedure. They are asking for law. The easiest, simplest way for a person to think is in a rule based, legalistic way. They have a problem, they want to know how to solve the problem and they want steps. So the reason people like steps is because it makes things simple and easy. Unfortunately steps don't always work as they don't address every situation. They are sometimes too simple. In praying for others we must use principles if we want total success.

Of course there is an opposite extreme, people who want no steps, no rules and no law. They claim to be "spiritual" and want nothing to do with rules, steps or guidelines. They feel that anything goes as long as it is "spiritual." They complain about laws and rules and say that we have total freedom when we are in the Spirit. They use verses like Romans 7:6:

> But now, by dying to what once bound us, we have been released from the law so that we serve in the new way of the Spirit, and not in the old way of the written code.

Yet God gave us rules, God gave us the law and the law is good. Psalms 1:1-3 says:

> Blessed is the man that walks not in the counsel of the ungodly, nor stands in the way of sinners, nor sits in the seat of the scornful.
>
> But his delight is in the law of the LORD; and in His law he meditates day and night.
>
> And he shall be like a tree planted by the rivers of water, that brings forth his fruit in his season; his leaf also shall not wither; and whatsoever he does shall prosper.

Psalms 119:160 says:

> All Your words [God's words] are true; all Your righteous laws are eternal.

In Romans 7:12, Paul says:

> The law is holy, and the commandment is holy, righteous and good.

God gave us rules and instructions and they are good. In fact, what these quotes above call the "law" is the very Word of God itself. The first five books of the Bible are collectively called the Torah and the word *Torah* means *Law* in Hebrew.[42]

In Jesus' day, when the Hebrew high priest walked around with a scroll tucked under his arm to read at the temple, that scroll was the Torah, it was the law. Effectively he was reading the law to the people. Every Sabbath day when the people came to listen to the readings of the Word of God they were listening to the law of God.

---

[42] The word *Torah* refers to the first five books of the Bible, but the word itself translates as *law, instruction,* or *direction.*

The Greatest Commandment

But Jesus revealed something that was being missed. Jesus revealed that the spirit behind the law was love. Matthew 22:34-40 says:

> But when the Pharisees had heard that He [Jesus] had put the Sadducees to silence, they were gathered together.
>
> Then one of them, which was a lawyer, asked Him a question, tempting him, and saying, "Master, which is the greatest commandment in the law [the torah]?"
>
> Jesus said unto him, "You shall love the Lord your God with all your heart, and with all your soul, and with all your mind.
>
> "This is the first and greatest commandment. And the second is like unto it, You shall love your neighbor as yourself. On these two commandments hang all the law and the prophets."[43]

As a little boy, I thought that the word *commandment* in this question only referred to the Ten Commandments and I was confused. But what the lawyer was really asking was, "In all of the law, in all of the Torah and the prophets, in all of the entire Old Testament, what is the most accurate sum total of the law? What one rule embodies the entire law? What is the culmination or the fulfillment of the entire Word of God?"

Jesus answered, "Love."

Love is the spirit behind the law. Love is what we are supposed to operate in. Jesus did not come to take away the law or to destroy the law but to reveal the spirit behind the law. Jesus came to show us how to operate in love. Love is the spirit behind the law. The spirit of the law is love. The law still exists and is good. The law is the Word of God. Jesus is the Word of God. Jesus is love. The spirit *behind* the law and *of* the law is love.

When this was first revealed to me I saw all the places that I was operating *exclusively* in a rule based, step-by-step system. So

---

[43] The Old Testament, as we know it, is composed of three groupings of writings or scrolls; the Torah, the Nevi'im and the Ketuvim. These three words translate as the *law*, the *prophets*, and the *writings* respectively. In the times of Jesus, the Ketuvim writings were not yet fully respected as inspired by all scholars, so many only referred to the first two scrolls, the *law and the prophets*.

many times I was operating in the letter of the law and not the spirit of the law and didn't even realize it. 2nd Corinthians 3:6 says:

> He has made us competent as ministers of a new covenant—not of the letter but of the Spirit; for the letter kills, but the Spirit gives life.

Let me rewrite this verse with my comments in brackets:

> He has made us competent as ministers of a new covenant—not of the letter [of the law] but of the Spirit [of the law]; for the letter [of the law] kills, but the Spirit [of the law] gives life.

We are to operate not in the letter of the law but in the spirit of the law. Jesus did not come to take away the law and replace it with spiritualism. The law is good and righteous. Jesus came to reveal the spirit behind the law. As it says above, if we operate in the letter of the law, without the spirit, it brings death. Operating in rules *alone* brings death. Operating in formulas *alone* brings death.

Yet, operating in a rule based, step-by-step system is so easy to do. It is the most natural, human way to operate.

For example if a person asks, "Please tell me how to get people saved." What they are usually looking for is a series of steps. They are desperate to see their loved ones receive the same grace that they received. Their hearts are sincere, but they are still thinking like a human. They are still trapped in a rule based, legalistic system of thinking. Unfortunately, so often they get just what they ask for, a series of steps. The answer is often these two steps, "Repent and say the sinner's prayer."

Yet, I have seen so many perform lists of steps which are supposed to get a person saved and then, afterwards, they are not changed. When a person receives Jesus they are supposed to become a new creation.[44] Something internal and supernatural is supposed to happen. They are supposed to be different.

Of course some *are* changed, but others are not. Some people go to the altar to be saved and return back to their seats unchanged. Some get baptized in water and go down a dry sinner and come up a wet sinner. In effect they are worse off than when they started be-

---

[44] 2nd Corinthians 5:17

cause they now *think* they are saved and are still sitting on that same rocket ship to Hell.[45]

We listed a few steps in earlier chapters as a foundation, but my experience is that lists of steps won't work for everyone. Just like repenting and saying the sinner's prayer will be enough for some but not all,[46] that simple framework of steps from our earlier chapters will work for some but not all. But we want all! We want to operate in a dynamic system that works for everyone. We are not satisfied with batting .400. We want a home-run every time! [47]

Back when I was exclusively following a set of rules, I was praying and people were mostly getting healed. I was using my steps that came straight from the Word of God. I was sincere and I saw some results. I wanted people to be healed back then just as much as I do now. Yet I was operating in legalism and following a set of steps and didn't even know it. I was operating in the letter of the law.

Later, as I matured, the Lord called me to operate in love; to operate in the spirit that is behind the law. I did not throw away my set of steps. These steps are a framework. Just as Jesus did not come to destroy the law but to show us the spirit of the law, the Lord God did not pull me away from the instructions that I found in His Word but gave me the spirit behind those instructions.

Practicing the Law

We can study the Word of God and based upon the lessons found therein we can put together a list of steps that would satisfy almost any goal. In my case, I attempted to learn everything there was to know about praying for people. I studied the Word and looked to the lessons from Jesus and the Apostles. I studied exactly how they prayed and I came up with a set of steps. I made my own personal list of rules on how to pray.

---

[45] See Matthew 23:15

[46] The core reason that it does not work for many is that they are performing these steps mentally. Faith is not released. The Spirit is not in it.

[47] For those unfamiliar with American sports, this is a reference to the game of Baseball. In Baseball, batting .400 is quite good and means that the batter got a hit 40% of the time.

What I learned in this study was taught to me directly by the inspiration of the Holy Spirit. I know that I learned from God because something supernatural was happening while I read. The letters on the page would grow bigger in my eyes. Certain passages seemed to stand out from others like there was an otherworldly light on the page. It was a spiritual illumination leading me to *see* certain things. It was a set of steps straight from God.

I then put these steps into practice. And they worked! People started to get healed. God was touching people and I saw the miraculous right in front of my eyes. I cried so hard because God was using me and it was beautiful. I never felt like I deserved such an honor. Why would God use me? I saw God move as people were healed of sickness, disease and emotional problems.

Then something peculiar happened. A few people walked away not healed.

The other prayer warriors responded defensively, "Sometimes God doesn't heal instantly," or, "Hold onto your faith and press in."

Those are true sayings, but something did not feel right inside. My heart was twisting.

Other times it was an emotional problem or an unemployed person looking for a job. After a few weeks their condition was the same or even worse. In my heart I knew something was left undone when we prayed. I knew something was not completed. I couldn't exactly put my finger on it, but I knew I had to learn more and progress. I had to pray better.

I prayed, "Lord, not all are receiving and I know that you promised to touch all. I must be failing You somewhere. Lord, give me some more steps.

"Teach me Father. What I am doing wrong? I want to see everyone get healed. Not only half. Not only 80% or 90%, but 100%. Lord, show me how to do it. Teach me, train me up, Lord. If I have to change then I'll change but give me more steps."

The Lord spoke, "It is not about more steps. It is not about more rules. It is not about more law or legalism. You need to operate in the spirit behind the law, the spirit behind the steps. You need to operate in love."

I contested, "Lord, I *do* love these people! I *do* have compassion for them! I so *desperately* want to see them get healed. I just don't know *what to do!*"

The Lord replied, "Ahhhh, exactly. You are looking for steps to do. It is not about *what to do*. You are not operating in love. You need to operate in love."

I reluctantly said, "Lord, I guess I don't know what that means. Teach me Lord."

The Woman at the Well

One of the ways God taught me is illustrated in the story of the woman at the well Let's look at how Jesus deals in love in this story. John 4 says:

5 So He [Jesus] came to a town in Samaria called Sychar, near the plot of ground Jacob had given to his son Joseph.

7 When a Samaritan woman came to draw water, Jesus said to her, "Will you give me a drink?"

9 The Samaritan woman said to him, "You are a Jew and I am a Samaritan woman. How can you ask me for a drink?" (For Jews do not associate with Samaritans)

Jesus answered her, "If you knew the gift of God and who it is that asks you for a drink, you would have asked Him and He would have given you living water."

"Sir," the woman said, "you have nothing to draw with and the well is deep. Where can you get this living water? Are you greater than our father Jacob, who gave us the well and drank from it himself, as did also his sons and his flocks and herds?"

Jesus answered, "Everyone who drinks this water will be thirsty again, but whoever drinks the water I give him will never thirst. Indeed, the water I give him will become in him a spring of water welling up to eternal life."

The woman said to him, "Sir, give me this water so that I won't get thirsty and have to keep coming here to draw water."

He told her, "Go, call your husband and come back."

"I have no husband," she replied.

Jesus said to her, "You are right when you say you have no husband. The fact is, you have had five husbands, and the man you now have is not your husband. What you have just said is quite true."

19 "Sir," the woman said, "I can see that you are a prophet."

25 The woman said, "I know that Messiah (called Christ) is coming. When he comes, he will explain everything to us."

Then Jesus declared, "I who speak to you am He."

Just then his disciples returned and were surprised to find him talking with a woman. But no one asked, "What do you want?" or "Why are you talking with her?"

According to the interpretation of the Torah by the Pharisees, Jesus was to have no contact with this woman as she would have been seen as unclean for a Rabbi. She was a Samaritan who had multiple husbands and she was alone. Jesus was considered to be a Rabbi, an authority on the law, a teacher of the ways of God. In Jesus' time, a Rabbi was to be righteous and separated off to God. A Rabbi was supposed to be an example to the people of pure, righteous and clean living. They were supposed to remain separated from unclean people. A Rabbi was supposed to be an example to the people, an example for the people to look up to. Jesus was not supposed to have contact with Samaritans, with unclean women, and especially not alone.

So Jesus was sitting in the thick of a powerful ministry with the Jewish people when he is shown in His spirit this lone woman afar off in this Samaritan city. His heart cried out to her. He loves her and needs to go minister to her.

Of course, according to the law what she needed was to repent. She was in sin and needed to repent from her lifestyle. If Jesus was operating fully and exclusively in the letter of the law then he could have walked up to this woman and screamed out at the top of his lungs, "Repent!" and walked away. Jesus would have been correct, just and righteous according to the letter of the law.

But Jesus did not do this. Jesus operated in love. Jesus operated in the spirit of the law not the letter of the law. Of course there is a balance also. Jesus not only loved *her*, but all the disciples and all people around Him and her. Jesus had to operate in such a way that by saving her, he did not lose others.

Jesus loved the disciples also and knew that they would get offended if they saw what he wanted to do. They were not high priests but they went to synagogue and knew the rules. They would have offense if they saw the One they followed going off to speak to a lone woman with loose morals, so Jesus sent them on an errand to go get food when He was not even hungry. He was just getting rid of them with a distraction. He did this in love. He did this to protect their delicate hearts from offense.

Next Jesus had to be concerned with all the townspeople of the Samaritan village. He could not deal with this woman publicly there. The townsfolk might become offended or the woman could be publicly embarrassed. He did not march into the city and call her out in the town square. He waited for her at the well. By spiritual revelation He knew that she would come there. This was all done in love.

When she arrived at the well, he does not yell out, "Repent!" He ministers to her. He starts off slow. He waits to catch her spirit. He starts a conversation with her and waits for His spirit to connect with her spirit. He is waiting on the Holy Spirit to start speaking to Him to reveal the thoughts and intents of the woman's heart. He is waiting for Holy Ghost spiritual discernment. He starts to touch her spirit and commune with her. He is dealing with her in love and revealing himself to her in baby steps.

So many times we have to deal with people in baby steps. Often God will reveal more than we should say. God will show us things so we can know how to deal with the situation, but will only tell us to say so much. He usually will tell us to say enough things so that the person knows that it is God, yet not so much that they are embarrassed. Do not air their dirty laundry on the public clothesline. Jesus did not blurt out to her that He was messiah before He even said, "Hello." He waited for revelation to strike her spirit first. Let God reveal to the heart first.

Another Example

This story of the woman at the well reminds me of an experience I had some years ago.

I remember the young man slowly stepping forward and asking to be "forgiven." He was in his early twenties with a relaxed look about him and he would not give me any other information.

Who knew what this man had actually done and what he wanted to be forgiven of?

The region was known for crime. The park grass that we stood on struggled to rise above the broken beer bottles and cigarette butts that littered the hard packed earth.

What had this man done? He only said that he wanted to be "forgiven for what he had done" as he stared at the floor and made circles in the dirt with his foot. He would not look me in the eyes.

Right then and there, I could have operated in legalism. I could have said, "According to the Word of God, your sins are forgiven. The blood of Jesus covers all of your sins and your sins are forgiven."

This would have been a correct statement. I would have been completely right and correct according to the Word of God but would not have helped him one little bit. I would have operated in the letter of the law and brought death upon his head. Then I could have continued, saying, "Go now and sin no more," as I sent him on his way. I would have been right with the law. I would have ministered in the letter of the law which brings death and not life.

⋅ I could have operated that way, but that is not what I did. I operated in love. Remembering Jesus with the woman at the well, I began to ask him questions. I was not searching for information to mentally "figure it out." I was just giving my spirit time to touch the supernatural. I asked him if he was saved and filled with the Holy Spirit.

Twice he said, "Yes."

In my natural mind this seemed like a paradox, he realized that his sins were already forgiven yet even after I explained this he was still standing there.

He squeezed my hand tightly. "You just have to pray for me," he said with a voice that suddenly revealed a hidden desperation.

I stopped asking questions and said, "Let's see what the Lord says," and started praying silently in front of him. I needed God to show me what was the real problem —obviously there was something more that this man was refusing to say.

Just then, God spoke to me. The man had an addiction, what he really needed was freedom from this addiction. Much more God told me. God revealed to me what the exact problem was and even what the man was thinking. John 13:19-20a, 30 says:

Jesus gave them this answer: "I tell you the truth, the Son can do nothing by himself; He can do only what He sees His Father doing, because whatever the Father does the Son also does. For the Father loves the Son and shows Him all He does."

"By myself I can do nothing; I judge only as I hear, and my judgment is just, for I seek not to please Myself but Him who sent Me."

This man was about to lose his wife and family if he continued on this path. His wife had given him an ultimatum. He was at the crossroads. God revealed the secret things. This man was at the showdown and he knew he couldn't do it on his own.

Now with this revealed knowledge, I did not then yell out, "You are exposed! I see your evil heart! I see your addiction! Repent!"[48]

Not at all. I softly said, "Brother, I see an addiction. But you can be free. The Lord Jesus can set you free from it."

I spoke to the man and told him what God had said. When a person hears the secret things of his or her heart spoken openly out in the air it does something. He knows that it is God. I never saw this man before in my life and may never see him again, yet God knew him. God told the truth of the matter right to his ears. It was a spiritual revelation. It was an unveiling. God ripped the blanket off the bed to reveal the naked man lying underneath, cold and bare. There is no hiding from God. His heart melted, he knew it was not a man reading his mind but God speaking to him through a man. He knew that this experience had nothing to do with me, it was God dealing directly with his heart.

Many times when you pray there is something in the way. There is something blocking a person's access to God. This *word of knowledge* will reveal what it is. A person may have depression, unconfessed sin, greed, or an unforgiving attitude. Many people who come to be prayed for do not consciously know what it is until God speaks it out loud, then their faces light up! They say, "*That is exactly it!*"

When God speaks it out, it is revealed, it is uncovered and the needy person sees it and knows it. Sometimes, it is as if they knew it all along. This man knew but at the same time he couldn't face it. he said he just wanted to be forgiven but it was freedom from addiction he really needed. He came to be prayed for but would not say exactly what for. God knew. God spoke it out and it was done!

---

[48] There are times when the Lord will tell us to deal harshly with people, but even then we must still do it in love.

"Brother, do you accept it? Do you accept the freedom that the Lord Jesus gives?" I softly whispered to him.

He accepted and we cast that addiction out of him. Just when we finished praying, I saw a dramatic change in his appearance. His speech changed from a barely audible whisper to a victorious yell! His posture and countenance changed. When he first entered, his head hung low and his shoulders drooped. He left leaping in the air, arms raised high! He was free! Jesus freed him! The addiction was gone.

He began to scream loudly, "It's done! It's done! It's done!"

Tears poured from his eyes because he was set free! The desire for the drug was completely removed from his heart. He did not want it anymore. He had no desire for it. He had no interest in it! I knew he would never do drugs again, not because he wanted to be holy or because he did not want to lose his wife and children. It was because the Lord completely removed all desire for drugs from his heart. He was free! He was free!

Boldness and Harshness

Operating in love does not necessarily mean always whispering and being gentle. I have already hinted that there are times when God calls for us to be stern or even harsh or hard.

I have seen people who were on the sidelines watching the prayer tent at an outdoor revival become upset because they saw something that they thought was too harsh or aggressive but if it is done in the love of God then it is perfect and what was required.

Once there was a demon possessed man who came to be delivered of a disease. He did not complain of a demon but only said that he was physically sick and wanted prayer. With spiritual eyes the source of the sickness was revealed. Some people are sick because of bacteria, virus or disease, others because of mental or emotional difficulties and the issue is psychosomatic, and still others are sick because of demons. This man had a demon and it was making him physically ill.

He came in begging and whimpering like a whiny baby, "Oh, it just hurts so bad! Oh, I am in so much pain!"

Inside I felt so terrible for him. I just pitied him. In retrospect, I think the demon was using this pity to immobilize us.

When one man tried to touch him to pray, he recoiled, "Oh, don't touch me! It hurts!"

Seeing the demon, that particular prayer warrior stepped back and took a full arm swing, slapping the man on the cheek. Hard!

I was surprised. Many were shocked. I didn't see that coming! Just then, the entire disposition of the man changed. He fell to the floor and hissed an evil hiss. He began to spit and curse in a low growl. Filth and foul poured from his mouth as the demon manifested. He began to rock back and forth on his hands and knees like a Jurassic carnivore ready to pounce.

The man of God pointed his finger at the man's nose and commanded the demon to leave. Just when it left the man rolled over and collapsed motionless. He was set free.

Thinking of this, another famous tale comes to mind. One of the most well-known ministers of healing that came out of the Pentecostal age of 100 years ago was Smith Wigglesworth. As the story goes, Smith was preaching on a stage and many were getting healed. A desperate woman ran up with her dead child in her arms, crying her eyes out. She placed the child on the stage at Smith's feet begging him to pray for her son. Smith turned and gave the child a tremendous football kick that sent the child across the auditorium. The crowd gasped in horror until the child landed on his feet and began running up and down the aisles.

Never do something like this unless God tells you to, but have the faith to do it when He does.

There are times for harsh words and harsh actions, but only when under the leading of the Holy Spirit. Had the child landed in the aisle still dead, Smith may have been joining him. But understand that harshness and boldness is sometimes the only way to effectively reach someone and free them from their problem. Understand God may call you to be harsh at times and that if you fail to follow through, the person may not receive.

To operate in love is to yield ourselves to the direction of the Holy Spirit and for us to be ready for anything the Holy Spirit will tell us to do. We should not just say some words and hope God takes care of it. We should try to do everything 100% right so that people receive 100% of the time. We should never be satisfied with some of the people getting healed while others are still wallowing in misery and hurt. God came to heal ALL. If there is a stronghold or a barrier, then we need to find out what it is and break it down.

We cannot take one set of rules or steps and apply them to every situation. Something that worked for us once may not be successful another time because there may be a barrier in the way. We must follow the leading of the Lord and seek His wisdom and discernment and do it in love.

Motive of the Heart

Dear saints of God do not be misled in what is being said here. It seems in this chapter that we are emphasizing the gifts of discernment that accompanies the prayer. And yes, it is so much easier to pray for people when the Holy Spirit comes and shows the exact problem and the direction to pray, but do not confuse these glorious gifts with love. Yes, supernatural things do happen and they are wonderful, but without love they are nothing. Without love, the strongest and most powerful gift can lead to confusion and death. First get God's love in your heart. Let God's love for people be the very motive of your heart and then the direction of all the supernatural that flows through you will be perfected and powerful. In 1 Corinthians 13:1-2, 13, Paul writes:

> If I speak in the tongues of men and of angels, but have not love, I am only a resounding gong or a clanging cymbal.
>
> If I have the gift of prophecy and can fathom all mysteries and all knowledge, and if I have a faith that can move mountains, but have not love, I am nothing. If I give all I possess to the poor and surrender my body to the flames, but have not love, I gain nothing.
>
> And now these three remain: faith, hope and love. But the greatest of these is love.

This perfect love is not the love of fellowman, love of husband and wife, or love of children but a godly love that we cannot know without God. It comes *only* from the Holy Spirit, and we must have the Holy Spirit *within us* to know this love. Yes, the gifts are vitally important, but as Paul states, the gifts can be misused by people who do not have godly love. He says that a person who "speak in the tongues of men and of angels" is a "resounding gong or a clanging cymbal" if they do it without God's perfect love inside of them – it is an "uncertain sound" that is false. Maybe you have great powerful gifts of God inside of you. Do not rely solely on them; rely on God and God's love. Paul says that if a person has a spiritual gift of faith he or she might not necessarily have God's love.

When Jesus described the true believers, He didn't say we would recognize them by their spiritual gifts, He said that we would recognize them by their love.[49] Have compassion for those you deal with. See them in God's eyes. Look at their problems through their own eyes. Jesus said that we must even love those who hate us.

Phileo, Eros, and Agape

Once, there was a man we were praying for who could not walk without a cane. He staggered forward on wobbly legs, barely able to stand. As we prayed for him nothing happened. I knew we were praying rightly, but we made no progress. Just then one of the pastors noticed the man's teenage son standing there.

He said, "Son, we need you to pray for your Dad."

The boy prayed with such a compassion for his father. He was directly affected and of course he wanted to see his dad healed for his own sake but there was something much deeper. He saw his father's pain and heartache first-hand everyday. He saw his father, a hard-working man, reduced to a cripple. He saw a man that wanted to provide for his family with every ounce of his being, reduced to relying on subsidies.

The boy prayed with fervency and compassion and the man was healed. He was restored. He released the cane and began to walk. At first two people held each arm as he walked. Then after a time only one person held one arm. Then no one held him up. The leg tremors left. He began to walk faster. He stepped boldly and quickly. He was touched by God!

The following day we were praying for a man with an eye disease. The same teenager was present and was praying with us.

Just then one of the prayer warriors said, "Son, now you pray right now for this man just like you did for your Dad. You pray for this man like he was *your* Dad."

Those words teach a lesson we should always try to follow. Always try to pray for children and young adults with the same compassion as if it was your own son or daughter. Always try to pray for

---

[49] John 5:42, John 13:34-35

adults with the same compassion as if it was your own sister, brother, father or mother. This compassion is good and helps tremendously.

The compassion we are discussing so far is good but godly love is so much more. Let's look at how godly love is different, special and so much more than compassion or brotherly love.

As many of you already know, there are three different Greek words, Phileo, Eros, and Agape (φιλεο, ερος, αγαπε) that all can be translated into English as *love* but each has a different shade of meaning. *Phileo* is commonly called *brotherly love* and is the love between friends or the love of our fellow man (human).[50] *Eros* is the *passionate love* between a husband and wife and *agape* is the *godly love* that is between God and humankind.[51]

The difficulty with operating in love is that the love that we must operate in is agape, yet almost no one has a full understanding of this type of love. Agape love is godly love and comes only from God. Only God can provide it. It has been my experience that when the Lord pours out agape through someone, man and woman alike sometimes misunderstand it and misinterpret it.

At times I have prayed for women and upon getting healed or delivered, they became enamored with me. I have treated these women with the same dignity, respect, and distance that I would a man. I do not look at them seductively or try to entice them. I have prayed long about this and according to the revelation of the Holy Spirit, I operated properly. My hands are clean of this. But I say this not as a confession but to warn all of us, male or female. The love of God can and will well up inside us if we allow it. We can feel such a deep compassion for people and their conditions. It is a compassion so deep that it is more than compassion, it is godly love. It is agape.

Now when God's love, the agape, pours out of us, the person we are praying for can feel it as if it was radiating out of us like the warmth of sunlight, but they may not understand it. They may not recognize what it is. They might not have experience with the love of God. In their heart, they feel the love of God radiating off of us and shining on them like the warm rays of sunshine that heats our face on a hot August day. It awakens something inside. But what

---

[50] Actually, there are two different types of phileo love, one is brotherly love and the other is family love, but you get the point.

[51] The word eros (ερος) is not found in the Bible.

they are feeling is so much more than the touch that took away the cancer or straightened the spine, they feel the love of God shining all over their insides. The rays of the sun strike the skin, the rays of the Son strike the spirit.

This is a caution. Be careful how much you receive from people –a sign of appreciation can turn into something more. Too many have fallen here. People feeling such a strong love naturally want to return it, to give it back. Yet they have no experience with agape and return what they know, they return eros or phileo love. They appreciate so much what they have received and want to shower love on us, but they only know the love of man. Be careful!

Not only do we need to be careful of others but ourselves also. We must look at our own hearts also. We must not confuse the agape God has placed in us with phileo or eros. We must analyze ourselves and make sure that the love that we feel and identify with is agape in our hearts.

If we have not mastered this then it can be especially difficult if the person we are praying for is attractive. We are all human and just because someone is beautiful or attractive does not mean that we are in lust. But again, this is a warning. Become a master of this and discern the source of it.

Remember that the love that wells up inside of us is of God. It is agape. It is the love of God inside of us that drives the compassion inside of us. Do not look at men or women in lust but in godly compassion driven by agape love.

This has been a recognized problem among Christians and many churches try to avoid it through legislation. Some make rules that men and women cannot pray for each other –even they cannot shake hands when greeting. Other places have the men and women sitting on different sides of the church. Of course this is legalism and does not deal with the true problem, the desire.

How did Jesus handle it? Lets look at Luke 7:36-47:

Now one of the Pharisees [Simon Peter] invited Jesus to have dinner with him, so he went to the Pharisee's house and reclined at the table. When a woman who had lived a sinful life in that town learned that Jesus was eating at the Pharisee's house, she brought an alabaster jar of perfume, and as she stood behind Him at his feet weeping, she began to wet his feet with her tears. Then she wiped them with her hair, kissed them and poured perfume on them.

119

When the Pharisee who had invited him saw this, he said to himself, "If this man were a prophet, he would know who is touching him and what kind of woman she is—that she is a sinner."

Then He turned toward the woman and said to Simon, "Do you see this woman? I came into your house. You did not give me any water for my feet, but she wet my feet with her tears and wiped them with her hair. You did not give me a kiss, but this woman, from the time I entered, has not stopped kissing my feet. You did not put oil on my head, but she has poured perfume on my feet. Therefore, I tell you, her many sins have been forgiven—for she loved much. But he who has been forgiven little loves little."

This sinful woman was touching and loving Jesus yet there was no carnal desire there. It was all pure. It was all agape love. Can we achieve this in this day? Yes, but I still recommend distance and caution so that we are never misinterpreted.

Pray with love. Pray with compassion. It is not about numbers, miracles, or great manifestations. It is about love for people. Deal with people in love. Deal with them in God's perfect love. We must keep our hearts right. The motive of our heart is the most important thing. We must say only what God shows us and what He releases us to say. God loves people in perfection and died for them. He knows how to deal in perfect love. Deal with people in God's perfect love.

Chapter 8

Preparation

Barely holding on to consciousness, barely able to stand, I watched in the distance in a solemn awe at what God had just done.

The young man couldn't stop smiling. He giggled like an innocent, five year-old silly girl dancing a silly girl dance in front of the entire family at the annual backyard cookout at grandma's house. Flailing his arms in the air in new-found victory, he jiggled around on his tiptoes before the Lord.

Me, I was spent. I was drained, but it brought me a soft, quiet joy to see him. As I stood there, bracing myself on the soft bark of that old maple tree, watching the kid celebrate his new found freedom, my mind drifted back over how it all had happened.

Only twenty years old, he had already spent over four years in prison for stabbing a man nearly to death. As I spoke to him, the face of Kurt Cobain on his shirt stared back at me and jeered, arm extended and middle finger up in a rebellious salute to anarchy. The young man had been a heroin addict and dabbled in witchcraft. Even he had sacrificed himself over to the darkness, inviting demons into his body. He had willingly given himself over to full possession. But I didn't know all that just yet.

Sometimes God shows you things in stages. Sometimes you do not see everything all at once. The young man eventually told us he was an addict and later gave up all the drugs in his pocket yet I detected that he was lying about something. I couldn't understand why he would be lying yet hand over all his dope. I did not initially see the demons, but I knew he was lying about something. I knew he was hiding something.

When he entered the park, the demons were speaking through him and he was so mixed up and confused that even he himself did not know which words were his own. Each time the boy spoke, I heard a distant laughter, like a far-away echo on the breeze that blew off the river. I strained to try to hear the babbling words from the laughing voices, strained to try to understand what was happening here. *Was I going crazy?*

I began to realize that it was demons laughing at us, taunting us. They were controlling his mind, making him lie, making him say what they told him to say and the demons thought that was hilarious. They were trying to make fools out of the Christians. What good sport!

The strange thing was that when the demons would speak through the boy they would say things that would sound right to a Christian. Some didn't see the lying spirits; they thought we were making good progress because they heard such good things come out of the boy's mouth, but it was all lies.

The boy said, "Yes, yes, I just need to keep myself surrounded by good Christian people like all of you," and then I heard the laughter in the wind, "Ha ha ha ha!"

"Oh yes, I will never do drugs again."

"Ha ha ha ha!"

"Oh, what you said just took my breath away! I feel changed and set free!"

The laughter in my ears was getting louder and closer, "Ha ha ha ha!"

He was lying. It was a demon just saying anything he could to get out of there and the boy didn't even know it. The boy trapped inside was being held captive. Because of these lies, some of the prayer warriors thought that we were successful. They saw him hand over his drugs -another great success for God!

The lying spirits would say anything to hold on, anything to just get out of there.

After a time I began to see them visually. Like misty illusions from some conjurer, they seemed to appear out of thin air, but the vision was dark, hazy and cloudy. As I stood behind the seated boy, I saw two black balls swirling around each other, leaving streaks of black, dusty mist behind them. One of them turned on its side and looked up at me and it was the ugliest face I have ever seen. It was like a round ball covered in thick, jet-black, wet hair. The hair was matted like it was wet with oil. At first I just saw the ball, but then it rolled over toward me as it spun in a circle and I saw it was a head. The red eyes were small and beady. The teeth were like wolf fangs and the mouth was oversized. The mouth took up over half of the head and could open very wide. I recalled seeing a nature program that explained how snakes can uncouple their jaws to open their mouths extremely wide. This demon had this kind of snake jaw. The mouth would open to twice the size of the head and bite into the side of this boy just below the ribs. He was using his teeth to hold onto the young man.

When I told the young man what I saw the blood drained from his face, becoming ashy pale. Then he looked at the ground and sheepishly confessed that he had invited them in. He even knew the demons by name. He closed his eyes, tilted his head back and started to softly sway as the demons rose up to take control of his body. Strong men pressed down on his shoulders and gripped his wrists, they seemed to know instinctively what was coming next.

We tried to pray them away, to cast out the demons, but they would not leave.

"We own him! Ha ha ha ha!"

They were invited in; they would not leave. His body swayed in larger and larger circles.

"Give up! He is ours!" The demons began to thrash and grind their teeth like metal bear traps being readied to spring on an unsuspecting foot in the woods.

As the young man started to recede deeper into himself, the strong demons started to slowly come out. A wrinkle of angry, demonic rage washed across his face, his eyes popped open and the flash of an oddly placed grin appeared, then, just as quickly, disappeared. The boy settled back into his chair, his body limp and head pointed back down as the men loosened their grip for just a moment. Quickly the demons tried to transition into control once more, his whole body tensed as his veins popped out on his arms, then just as quickly relaxed as the men grabbed hold tighter.

This was nothing like those stupid Hollywood movies where people's heads spin around and their skin turns green and bumpy. He looked physically no different than any other man of his age, it was only the expressions on his features and his mannerisms that changed.

Looking down at the many hands holding him down, he suddenly said plainly, "I feel like I want to jump up and hit you. All of you. I want to jump up and shred this tent with my bare hands." He didn't use some demonic, Hollywood-style, growly voice. He actually stated it kind of matter-of-fact just as if he was talking about the news or the weather, but inside the demons were deadly serious.

They were trying to get us to let our guard down but the boy couldn't help but relate what the demons wanted to do. Their minds were almost one.

Although the demons were now speaking out-loud, I could still see the trapped little boy inside. He looked up and smiled at me like a sweet innocent child. The young man was suddenly back again but I knew that if we let him go he would certainly destroy. It was only the several strong men that held him back.

It was all we could do to keep the young man's mind in front and prevent the demons from taking full control. As they tried to come back out and take control once again, we began to scream at him, "Don't you give up! Don't go into yourself! Don't let them take control! You can win this! You can be free!"

The police officer directing traffic at the revival entrance got nervous and started walking slowly toward us. After coming almost halfway, he paused for a few seconds, probably thinking twice about what he could do, and went back to his post.

The young man and the demons took turns being in control over and over, then, after over two hours in the deliverance tent, the young man was set free. The violent demons finally left him and he was free.

It was a long journey getting to that point. Many had fasted before this particular series of meetings and we established a forty-eight hour prayer chain. Someone in our group was always praying for forty-eight hours non-stop up until the moment the event started. No move of God comes without it being bathed in prayer.

On the night before the first meeting we all met for three hours of solid anointed prayer. There were about fifty of us. The anointing was so strong. God was there. I felt like I was soaking wet and it was dripping off of me. Many of the others told me they felt like they were exploding. They said it was almost too strong to bear.

Normally when I pray for a person, it takes some time before the true discernment comes and I see where the unseen blockage is and how to proceed. This time I was so full it was coming after seconds not minutes or tens of minutes. Everywhere I looked I saw visions. Thursday night we were so on-fire and full of power. There was a long string of powerful deliverances, healings, and salvations.

I slept very little, I was up all night thinking about it, smiling and enjoying the victory.

Friday began in the same manner until I faced the young man possessed of the demon. After working with him for about ninety minutes I started to feel worn down and weak. Another prayer warrior relieved me and I wandered over to the second prayer tent.

"Maybe I could pray for needs that were not so taxing," I thought.

People were also getting healed in the second tent. God straightened out one man's spine and removed all the pain from another's shoulder. Yet with each person it was becoming harder and harder for me.

At first the anointing was dripping off of me and it flowed freely. I was overflowing. After a time, I felt like I had to squeeze it out.

Next a man with acute vasculitis was healed. It is a disease that weakens all the blood vessels of the body, preventing them from supplying adequate blood to the organs and tissues. He had constant pain and weakness. He could not work or provide for his family. No treatment was effective and his doctors had given up on him. They even denied him a heart bypass operation because the veins of his heart were too fragile, he said. His skin was yellowish and pale; there was no apparent blood in his skin. As we prayed for him, he said he felt rings of fire radiating up through his feet and through his body. As the rings moved up, the pain decreased. Once the fire reached his heart all the pain in his body was gone.[52] Just then, I opened my eyes and looked at his face. I saw the blood enter his face and his cheeks became rosy. He started to smile and laugh. The pain was gone, his blood was flowing, and he was a new man.

Seeing such things first hand makes you want to see it again and again. I so wanted to see people delivered and healed. I began to reach deep inside of my belly and squeeze, spiritually. It flowed down my arms and into the person and they would get healed but there was less and less each time. It was like that verse in John 7:38 where Jesus says:

Whoever believes in Me, as the Scripture has said, "Rivers of living water will flow from within him."

---

[52] This was his description, not mine.

Yet, I began to struggle. Another came in and I squeezed again but there was not much left, just a trickle. I felt dizzy, I couldn't do it anymore.

I tried to direct the other less experienced prayer warriors in what to do. For a moment, it was like I was conducting an orchestra and I was using their anointing. They were the instruments. I started to get more and more light headed. I felt like I couldn't talk straight. I was trying to pray for someone but I couldn't get the words right. It was like I was having a stroke. I couldn't talk right. I was introducing confusion. Without realizing it, I began to squeeze out too much. I had given too much.

We must be so careful of our anointing and our spiritual state. We must be so careful to be fully prepared when entering into battle. I know now that people can pull things out of you. People can siphon away your anointing and even your strength. Sometimes this is not intentional, other times it is. When people are so hungry and have a need they can get desperate. It is like the woman who touched the hem of Jesus garment without asking permission. She was so desperate to be free of her condition! He said power left Him. Jesus was weakened. Luke 8:43-47 says:

> Now a woman, having a flow of blood for twelve years, who had spent all her livelihood on physicians and could not be healed by any, came from behind and touched the border of His garment. And immediately her flow of blood stopped.
>
> And Jesus said, "Who touched Me?"
>
> When all denied it, Peter and those with him said, "Master, the multitudes throng and press You, and You say, 'Who touched Me?'"
>
> But Jesus said, "Somebody touched Me, for I perceived power going out from Me."
>
> Now when the woman saw that she was not hidden, she came trembling; and falling down before Him, she declared to Him in the presence of all the people the reason she had touched Him and how she was healed immediately.

I was trying to use the anointing of the others but the needy were still pulling it out of *me* and I didn't recognize it. As they looked into my eyes with desire and need, they were draining me. I started to do more damage than good because of my own confusion.

126

I couldn't think anymore. I couldn't speak right anymore. A misty haze entered my head. I had to get out of there. Without saying a word I walked out of the tent and towards the crowds near the front.

I still did not realize exactly what was happening, *Maybe I am just too tired,* I thought.

The Lord was teaching me a hard lesson, first hand. I tried to help one more; a young lady at the front, praying by the musicians. Almost immediately another man interrupted us and stepped in. I didn't know him, he was not with us, but in my confused mind he seemed to know what he was saying and was sincere so I let him join us. My head was still cloudy and I could barely stand. This man went on and on, speaking for a really long time and when I tried to add something he basically told me to shut up, but in an almost polite way. Maybe he was right to bark me down as I was in such a state of confusion but as the young lady walked away discernment revealed that her problem remained with her. We had not attended to her need.

Offense jumped on me in my weakened state. Instead of a strong man of God that commanded sickness to flee, I became as an angry mouse with nothing to say.

Tomorrow I would spend much of the morning repenting and being restored. I learned such a valuable lesson. It seems that I am like many people who can be told something but not truly *know it* until they have *experienced it* first hand. People see the prayer warriors doing such mighty works but we are only human. We make mistakes too. We are always learning too. I would spend much of the next day dwelling on what had happened, praying, and learning. God would show me and teach me new things.

But tomorrow was another day. For now, I leaned against the soft bark of that old maple tree as the quiet breeze rustled my hair and I watched him. Barely able to stand I watched the young man celebrate. Slow tears rolled down my left cheek as I watched the once demon-possessed boy who God had set free.

Preparation

Preparation is so vital for the prayer warrior. No one goes unprepared into a battle if lives are at stake. Understand that not only can the lives of the people you pray for be at stake but the ones around you and your very own. I have seen demons manifest and a possessed person rise up in inhuman strength. Four grown men could barely hold down the possessed boy in the previous story. It is not a game and never a joke. Demons are certainly not in this for your entertainment.

Not long ago I was in church praying a few hours before service when the Holy Spirit fell on me. My entire body started shaking uncontrollably. I was freezing! I felt the cold hand of death descending upon me.

The Lord spoke to me, saying, "GET READY!" Someone who was suicidal was going to enter the church that morning and I needed to pray for her He told me.

I heard these very words, "It is a matter of life and death and her life is in your hands today. You only have one shot. That is all. GET READY!"

I was a bit nervous. Terrified actually. I have no fear of demons. I have no fear that the Lord will not come through. My concern was that I was going to make a mistake. I got serious and got ready and it happened just as He said it would.

I was standing near the church entrance a few hours later, greeting people as they came in when a woman with a half-crazed look walked past the others, directly up to me and asked me to pray for her saying, "I can't handle this anymore!"

By relating these things I am not trying to scare you away from praying for people, I am just trying to emphasis that this work is serious. It is also beautiful, wonderful, rewarding and full of joy but it is not a joke. Lives can hang in the balances.

Overview

Preparation is a huge topic and with only one chapter, we are only going to cover four distinct areas of preparation. Obviously there are many other things we could write about, unfortunately there is not time and space to discuss everything possible to prepare for.

Our first sub-topic on preparation then is to have a strong and constant relationship with God which only comes through long hours of prayer. So many people want to pray with authority, cast out demons, and bless their loved ones. Yet, they only spend a few moments alone with God each day. How do you expect to pray with God's authority when you do not spend any time with God? That doesn't even make sense.

Second, we will talk a bit about fasting and how that it can help tremendously in the harder cases. When I know in advance that I am going into a battle, I always fast. Even if it is just for a day. It seems that my spiritual fight is always stronger, my sword is always sharper, and my sight always keener when I am on an empty stomach.

Next, we will look at how authority is affected by permission. When you go to pray, you do not kick the doors in and march your troops into someone's living room. Always ask permission. Always make sure that the person you are praying for has a will that is in line with yours. God will not go where He is unwelcome and uninvited. God is a gentleman and always respects the will. God does not force you to be saved, neither does He force you to be healed.[53]

Finally, we will look at the important role of the intercessor. When we go into battle, whether it is at a camp meeting, an open-air prayer meeting at the parks, or just praying for someone at the altar call in church, it is always good to have someone in intercession. The intercessors help you reach the throne of God. You would be amazed at how effective your prayers are when you have a few intercessors gathered around praying for you and the effort.

One-on-One Time

So the first of these four sub-topics is spending one-on-one time with God. The number one most important thing that you can do, and the thing that the devil wants to prevent above all else, is spending one-on-one time with God.[54] The number one most important thing that you can do with your time is spend it in prayer, in communion with the almighty God.

When we say "spending one-on-one time with God," we must make a distinction because many people do not know how to pray or even how to read the Bible. There is a huge difference between saying a prayer and praying. There is a huge difference between reading

---

[53] Believe it or not I have met people who did not want to be healed. One man did not want to lose his disability check. If he was healed he would have to go back to work and he did not want that.

[54] This seems like a bold and possible incorrect statement. Many people would hold that reading the Word and praying have at least equal weight and maybe this is true if the anointing of the Holy Spirit is on you while you are reading. But too many people read the Bible like it is any other book and never pray.

the Bible "like a book" and reading the Bible under the anointing. The anointing of the Holy Spirit is what makes the difference. When a person prays, the Holy Spirit should be there and inhabiting your prayers.

When people pray *properly*, they have the anointing of the Holy Spirit on them. The anointing of the Holy Spirit enters the room and He reveals Himself. One preacher called it "entering the Holy Spirit Zone." The way the Holy Spirit chooses to reveal Himself to you does not matter, only that He does it.

Now, do not seek after feelings, emotions, sensations or supernatural experiences. Seek after Christ and the experiences *follow*. We should not seek after the fruit of the Spirit, but seek the Spirit Itself and the fruit will *follow*.

Many people say things like, "I am seeking after the joy of the Lord!" and on the surface that sounds like an acceptable statement, but really we should seek after Christ and the joy follows. Seek after the Holy Spirit and the manifestation of the Holy Spirit will follow. Do not seek after the result! Seek after the source and the result will follow.

And what are the results we are looking for? Preparation. God will prepare us. When a person is in prayer, the Holy Spirit will come and work on us. God will prepare us. Seek God and you will get the result.

In John 14:26, Jesus says:

> But the Comforter, which is the Holy Ghost, whom the Father will send in my name, He shall teach you all things, and bring all things to your remembrance, whatsoever I have said unto you.

And Romans 2:29 says:

> But he is a Jew, which is one inwardly; and circumcision is that of the heart, in the spirit, and not in the letter; whose praise is not of men, but of God.

And Colossians 2:11 says:

> In Him you were also circumcised, in the putting off of the sinful nature, not with a circumcision done by the hands of men but with the circumcision done by Christ

When we spend one-on-one time with God, the Holy Spirit will be present and He will start to work on our spirit. He will comfort. He will teach and He will circumcise. He will prepare you for the battle. He will cut away things and add in other things. Perhaps, you will not feel any different *physically* or think any different *mentally* because this operation is not necessarily on the mind or the body, but on the spirit. Spend time with God! It is the most important thing you can do! He will change your spirit. God knows what you will face. God sees the arsenal arrayed on the battlefield.

The Holy Spirit will work on you and changes will take place. This generally does not happen all at once in one big prayer session but every time you pray the Spirit will work out a little more. This is something that you should do everyday. Set aside a certain time and make that the Lord's time. Pray until the Holy Spirit falls and let Him work on you.

The Lord has also taught me many lessons on prayer in watching the ministries of others. I am not endorsing any specific ministry in this book, but I would like to share lessons I learned by observing. In 2008, there was a nationally televised revival in Lakeland, Florida that lasted over 100 days. The revival was lead by a Canadian evangelist named Todd Bentley. As I watched him, I pondered how he was able to continue, day after day, walking in such power and authority. How was he being restored? They had two services a day with the second one lasting as long as six hours.

Todd said that no matter the pressures or how much people were pulling on him that he locked himself away with God before he went on stage. He locked himself away, alone with God for at least three hours a day, right before the second meeting, everyday. If he did not do this, he did not go out. No cell phones. No computer. No interruptions. It was this one-on-one time that restored him. It was this one-on-one time that recharged his spirit, rejuvenated him and empowered him to continue the work.

Remember, when you pray, life will be drained out of you. Remember Jesus felt virtue leave Him when the women touched the hem of His garment. You must be restored. Spend one-on-one time with God to be restored. Prayer is the life line to God. Prayer is the umbilical cord. God is life and light and to be filled with that life and light we must spend time in prayer, locked away, alone with God.

I am not going to tell you how much to pray each day but I will tell you that the more time you put in alone with God, the more

131

authority you will walk in and the more results you will see. As for the lesson I learned from the story at the beginning of the chapter, it is clear to me that I should have spent several hours in prayer that morning. I didn't. We spent three hours praying the night before the Thursday gathering and great things happened. Friday morning I woke up physically exhausted so I didn't pray. I just went off to the meeting and I learned a hard lesson there. I believe that if I had approached each day as a new battle then things would have been different.

Get prepared. Get full of God's Spirit by spending time in prayer. Get alone with God and get full of Him. You will be more full of God's life. You will be more full of God's light and love. You will be able to pour out more to the needy when you pray.

As a young man I remember often singing an older song in church called *Sweet Hour of Prayer*.[55] Apparently back when this song was written it was considered normal to pray for at least one hour everyday. Prayer-minded families would gather together at home, not to watch television, but to pray together for an hour every night. I do not know where that mindset has gone, but so many people tell me that they, "Talk to God all day long" but when you really press them they say they only lock themselves alone with God for five minutes or not at all. Here is a portion of the song:

Sweet hour of prayer! sweet hour of prayer!
That calls me from a world of care,
And bids me at my Father's throne
Make all my wants and wishes known.
In seasons of distress and grief,
My soul has often found relief
And oft escaped the tempter's snare
By thy return, sweet hour of prayer!

Sweet hour of prayer! Sweet hour of prayer!
The joys I feel, the bliss I share,
Of those whose anxious spirits burn
With strong desires for thy return!
With such I hasten to the place
Where God my Savior shows His face,

---

[55] Sweet hour of Prayer was written by William Walford in 1845

And gladly take my station there,
And wait for thee, sweet hour of prayer!

Everyone wants the results! Everyone wants to walk in signs and wonders. Are you willing to put in the time for those results? Are you willing to give God the sacrifice of praise to get results?

Fasting

Our second topic in this chapter is fasting and I want to relate to you how I learned the dramatic importance of it through a story.

Before one large meeting, a forty day fast was called. Each individual could choose what they wanted to fast, it did not have to be food necessarily, but the idea was to get into a mindset of prayer and preparation.

At this time, I was ignorant of this principle so I did not take this fasting business too seriously. I had already completed a forty-day fast at the beginning of the year and I really was not looking forward to another so soon. I love to eat.

Additionally, I felt like I could handle my responsibility. I was only going to work in the prayer tent. I wasn't running the entire event or speaking up front. In ignorance, I felt like I had a minor, somewhat unimportant role. I had prayed for people before, I felt like I knew how to pray for people, and I felt like I was ready to pray for people at any moment. I didn't feel like I had to get ready for something that I do all the time anyway.

The Lord allowed me to go on with this wrong thinking for quite a while. Six days before the event He spoke to me. While I was in prayer, God told me to read the 10th chapter of Daniel then He explained it to me and explained why I was in error.

The 10th chapter of Daniel tells the interesting story of how Daniel was visited by an angel. Before the angel came, *something* was revealed to Daniel. Once this something was revealed, he immediately began fasting and praying. Daniel 10:1-3 says:

> In the third year of Cyrus king of Persia a thing was revealed unto Daniel, whose name was called Belteshazzar; and the thing was true, but the time appointed was long: and he understood the thing, and had understanding of the vision. In those days, I, Daniel was mourning [fasting] three full weeks. I ate no pleasant bread, neither came flesh nor

wine in my mouth, neither did I anoint myself at all, till three
whole weeks were fulfilled.

One of the things revealed to Daniel was that he needed to prepare for a spiritual battle. God anointed Daniel to fast because the
coming battle was going to be hard! The strongest forces of darkness
were going to bring their full arsenal against Daniel and serious spiritual preparation was necessary.

After three weeks of fasting an angel appeared and spoke to
Daniel. And what does the angel say?

He basically says, "I would have been here sooner, but I had
to fight the forces of darkness all the way here. In fact, the dark
forces were trying to prevent me so much that I had to return for rein-
forcements in order to reach you. I had to bring stronger angels with
me so that we could fight off the dark forces to reach you." Daniel
10 continues:

Then he [the angel] said, "Fear not, Daniel: for from the
first day that you set your heart to understand and to chas-
ten yourself before God, your words were heard, and I am
come because of your words. But the prince of the kingdom
of Persia withstood me twenty one days. Then Michael
came to help me. He is one of the leaders of the angels. He
helped me win the battle over the king of Persia."

Here are some points concerning this passage. First, the angel
was sent out from heaven immediately. Daniel's prayer was heard
immediately! As soon as Daniel did what God was calling him to do,
fast and pray, the angel from heaven was released and sent on his
mission. But even great and mighty angels have to war and fight and
some angels are stronger than others. We know that the angel Michael is one of the strongest. It took his strength to finally overcome
the forces of darkness.

There is a spiritual world. Many unseen battles are going on in
this spiritual world and we have control over their outcomes based on
actions we take. It seems odd to think that a human praying or fasting can release the power and force of mighty angels to do work, but
according to the Bible, that is how it works. Jesus purchased the authority over death and darkness with His blood and *gave* it to us as a
free gift. We have authority! The angels are subject to us! Demons
are subject to us!

But sometimes a spiritual battle is tough. That is why God anointed Daniel to fast and pray before his battle. That is why God anointed us to fast and pray before our battle.

Some would argue that this situation was only for the Old Testament and that it could not occur today. But there is a similar case in the New Testament where the disciples were having a hard time casting out a demon and Jesus told them to fast. Matthew 17:14-21 says:

> And when they were come to the multitude, there came to him [Jesus] a certain man, kneeling down to him, and saying, "Lord, have mercy on my son: for he is lunatic and sore vexed: for often times he falls into the fire, and oft into the water. And I brought him to your disciples, and they could not cure him."
>
> And Jesus rebuked the devil; and he departed out of him: and the child was cured from that very hour.
>
> Then came the disciples to Jesus apart, and said, "Why could not we cast him out?"
>
> And Jesus said unto them, "Because of your unbelief: for verily I say unto you, If you have faith as a grain of mustard seed, you shall say unto this mountain, 'Remove hence to yonder place,' it shall remove, and nothing shall be impossible unto you. Howbeit this kind goes not out but by prayer and fasting."

This is not to say that we need to fast in order to gain a victory. Jesus already obtained the victory. The battle itself is already won. We need to pray and fast to feed our faith, to increase our faith. Jesus said that they failed only because of unbelief. Their faith was insufficient. And what was required to increase their faith? Jesus said they needed to pray and fast.

In our case, God knew our spiritual battle would be beyond the measure of faith that we had. God knew we needed to increase our faith. The battle was already won at Calvary, but our faith had to increase. The only battle we have to fight is the battle of standing. The battle is a battle of believing, a battle of faith. God anointed us to pray and fast, just like Daniel, in preparation for battle, in preparation for victory.

I had failed to prepare for thirty-four days. Now, I had to get ready and do it quickly. I dedicated as much time as I could every single day to prayer, praising, and worshiping. And I began to fast. I was spending almost the entire day in the Spirit. I wanted to spend as much time as possible in God's presence and in His Spirit so that God's Spirit could make me ready for what was to come.

I had repented of my lack of preparation. I asked God to prepare me and make me ready. Only God knew what was really ahead and what type of preparation was needed. I submitted myself to the Holy Spirit to change me, correct me, mold me, make me, and fix me into the warrior I needed to be for this upcoming battle. I stayed in His Spirit in faith that He would do the work that I asked and submitted to Him to do.

I cannot say exactly what was changed or when. I cannot say exactly how I was different. Yet, I *knew* I was different. I had a confidence and boldness. I had a knowing. I *knew* there was no demon that could stand in my path. I was prepared!

Permission

Our third subtopic in this chapter is on permission. We should always gain permission for all of our actions from those who have authority over the area or person we are dealing with.

Remember, God is a gentleman. The Holy Spirit is a humble spirit. God does not force healing or any other type of freedom on anyone and then we cannot successfully petition God on behalf of a person without his or her permission.

As a prayer warrior,we must always have permission, agreement, and acceptance for every action that we take. We must always verify that the person that we are praying for agrees with how we are going to pray before we pray. We must always make sure that they have yielded authority to us.

If we are praying for people at an altar call or in a prayer tent in an outdoor tent revival, then just by entering the tent or approaching the altar, the person is requesting prayer and we have a certain level of authority. On the other hand, I have been led to pray for people in towns, on street corners, and in stores at times. Once the Lord gave me a word for a complete stranger who was working the checkout line at Burger King. We have to be very careful how we proceed in these kinds of situations. We should humbly approach them and respectfully tell them what the Lord has given us and ask permission. If they refuse, then that is fine, move on. We should never force ourselves on anyone –if we do, then our prayers probably won't be very effective anyway.

At an altar call it may be as simple as asking, "Can I pray for you?" In other situations, maybe in a store for example, we just have to introduce ourselves and tell the person what we are seeing or feeling. We should establish a connection with the person first. If they refuse, we shouldn't get offended, just move on.

Now once we have permission to pray, we should always make sure the person we are praying for agrees with the *direction* of our prayers. Many times, what the Lord shows is different than what the person asks for. If so, we should always tell the person what we see and ask them if they will allow us to pray for what we have seen. I have yet to have someone refuse, but this is not about being rejected, this is about authority. To gain authority over the situation we must have the agreement of the person we are working with.

This concept of permission also extends to locations. If praying for a person in a home, always ask permission of the owner of the house before beginning. This is very important, never wait to right before praying to get this permission, always do it as soon as possible, even right when entering the home.

In public spaces it is probably not always possible or necessary, but we should do it if we can. In an open air tent meeting or a revival campaign for example, it is always good to get a representative from the city or region to come and say a few words to open the meeting. Ask them to invite the Holy Spirit into the town and region. Ask them to open up their city and region for a move of God. By doing this we are gaining authority over the region and we will be much more successful.

To walk in great power, we cannot kick the doors down and claim victory. Authority is affected by our level of permission. God is a gentleman. Always ask permission. Always make sure that the person we are praying for has submitted to the move of the Holy Spirit. Ensure that they are yielded to receive. God will not go where He is unwelcome and uninvited. God always respects the will.

A special case for gaining permission applies to young children as well. When praying for children, it is important for the parents to know exactly what is going on. Ask them to join in praying, even if they are unsaved. The parents of the child have authority over their child. The permission we need is not necessarily from the child, especially if very young, but from the parents.

Mark 9:17-24 tells a story of a man who brings his son to Jesus to be healed. Jesus tells the father of the child, "If you can believe, all things are possible to him that believes." Notice that Jesus
speaks to the father, not to the child who is sick. Jesus does not address the faith of the child, but the faith of the father. The father has
the authority as the child is very young. When we pray for children
who are young, the faith, permission and authority of the parent
stands in for the child.

Here is another example. Many years ago, my oldest son was
very sick with an ear infection. It was the middle of the night and the
three year-old was howling in pain. Because it was the weekend and
our local hospital was notorious for their six-hour weekend lines at
the emergency room, I thought it better to take him to the family doctor in the morning. Meanwhile, I crawled into his bed with him and
started to pray for his ear. I knew that it would be my faith only that
would reach out and touch the hem of Jesus' garment. I prayed continually until my mind got out of the way and my faith rose up. My
son had been howling and whimpering in pain the whole time. All of
a sudden there was a perfect calm and silence in the room. My son
was instantaneously and completely healed. He was not howling,
moaning or whimpering anymore. There was silence.

He rolled over, looked at me and said, "Daddy, what happened?"

I said, "You were healed by Jesus."

He said, "*OK,*" rolled over and fell asleep.

The next morning he was up and playing. Everything was
back to normal.

Intercession

The final topic of this chapter is intercession. Intercessory
prayer is a little different from the type of prayer we have been discussing so far, so I will explain it through comparison.

When we normally pray and spend one-on-one time with
God, the Holy Spirit will come down and work on us, changing us,
comforting us, teaching us, quickening us, and circumcising us, but
when we are in intercession, we have dedicated that time for the Holy Spirit to do a work, not on us, but on the person or situation we are
praying for.

What happens in prayer is that the result are mostly dependent upon the level of faith that we have. In intercessory prayer, we are giving over our faith to help the person or situation we are praying for. It is like faith has a cumulative effect. It adds up! If you have ten people praying who all have a little bit of faith for example, all their individual amounts of faith add up to a larger amount.[56] So then if intercessors are surrounding a situation in prayer, it is much more likely to be successful.

If we have the blessing to be praying for someone when there are others around it is always a good practice for the others to be in intercession. This is something that should be almost instinctive in our churches. Everyone should know to do this right away without even being told.

We may not be directly working with someone or praying for someone, but as we stand on the sidelines we should be in intercession. The prayers of the intercessors support the work being done. We should never just sit back and watch the show! God's work is not here for spectacle and entertainment. Join in! Be in prayer of intercession for the great work being done.

It may not look like very important work, standing on the sidelines and praying, but it is one of the most vital things that can be done. The intercessor's faith joins with the faith of the others in the thick of the battle and mighty works are done.

This is not only my own personal lesson but the lesson that many great prayer warriors have learned. When I study the lives of the great prayer warriors of the past, one of my favorites who I always come back to is William Branham. He had one of the most dynamic and powerful of all the healing ministries of the 20th century.[57] He knew the power that came from intercession. Look what he says here:

> Someone said to me, "Brother Branham, where does this come from? How are you able to go meeting after meeting, staying under the anointing? Even one sign made Jesus weak when the woman touched His garment. I seen you stand for an hour under that."

---

[56] Some people say that it is actually much more like multiplying than adding.

[57] My opinion of course.

I said, "I'd like to tell you. Here's where it lays: he don't want me to say this, but my brother sitting here, Gene Goad, that boy don't touch bread or water for days, fasting and praying. Here sits Pat Tyler, this other brother sitting here by him. These men lay on their faces without food and water when I'm in a meeting, praying for me. That's where it comes from. If there wasn't something like that, I'd go down."

That's the men behind the curtain. The men who pray for strength in a message, they lay down everything. Maybe they haven't got the gifts to do those things [the signs, wonders, and miracles], but they're putting every effort they can to support it. The only way they know is prayer before God and fasting. There's where the power lays: let someone pray for you."[58]

William Branham had one of the most power healing ministries ever recorded and this is how he says it happened. At every meeting, when he was on the stage, he had people behind the stage curtain praying and fasting. This is where his power base was located.

I cannot stress enough the importance of having a great team together when you enter into these types of battles. When we go into a battle, we want to be surrounded by warriors. If we are going to war, we want fully armed and equipped, battle-ready warriors at our side.

I hope that this chapter has enlightened you on a few areas of preparation. The next few chapters deal more directly with the actual praying and provide more intimate experiences in praying for people. Hopefully you are beginning to see how to be led of the Holy Spirit as you pray and rely less on any sort of step-by-step legalistic method.

---

[58] William Branham said this during a sermon called "Be Not Afraid" preached on June 9th, 1960 in Chautauqua, Ohio. The above quote was edited slightly for clarity in printing. You can read a transcript of the original full sermon at www.branham.org.

Chapter 9

Discernment

There was death in this park. Drug dealers, broken bottles, gang members, cigarette butts, and empty drug vials owned this place. It was a place that the good citizens of this county avoided and referred to politely as a "bad neighborhood." Even nature seemed to reflect the condition of death that enveloped the park. The trees had a half-dead look of late autumn. The birds had gone away. They would not come here. The faded earth was hard packed. The bare, withered trees looked as if they were longing for the coming of December snow. Yet it was July.

Large metal poles protruded from broken and crumbling concrete searching to support the nonexistent wood planks that would make a fine bench for a pregnant mother watching her children play. But there were no planks except a lone rebellious standout that yet refused to be broken, a lone standout etched with the scars of gang names and profanity.

I scanned the horizon noting the few who had showed up to pray, to sing, and to bring the word of God to this blighted area. Many were asked to come but few arrived. Maybe fear kept many away? It is unfortunate that they did not come as they missed seeing a great work of God. I have noticed that when a stand is made for God that the greater adversity produces the greater results. When the enemy comes in strong, God rises up a standard and the glory falls.[59] Somehow I knew that the glory would surround this place today.

Staring at the dry and crumbling leaves lying still on the ground I thought, *"Not even the wind lives here."*

The chain link fence surrounding the small park trapped those inside like prisoners. Or was it to keep others out?

---

[59] Isaiah 59.19 says, "Do shall they fear the Name of the Lord from the west, and His glory from the rising of the sun; when the enemy comes in like a flood, the Spirit of the Lord will lift up a standard against him."

There was no line at the prayer tent so we began to walk around and talk to the people, to invite them and to show ourselves available to help.

About an hour later people started to come in after seeing one man who had come into the park on crutches jumping in the air, running around on his new legs and celebrating just as his wife was carrying the crutches to put them away in the car. Something was going on and God was moving too strongly.

A man and woman shuffle-stepped into the prayer tent and both asked for prayer saying the same few words. They both said they were seeking a closer walk with God. They both said that they were seeking God's direction. They said very little, only a few words each.[60]

I began to pray for the man first, asking God to show me what the problem was or how to pray. I had no idea what to say to such a vague request. They were "seeking God's direction." What was I supposed to say to that?

As God began to reveal things, I saw laziness in the man's spirit. I could see backslidden-ness all over him. It was God showing me what needed to be taken care of. Guilt draped over him like a thick, wet blanket. He was embarrassed of his condition and that is why he said so little. I saw that he knew exactly what to do and where he should be in his Christian walk but he just hadn't been doing it.

I did not know him so I wanted to be gentle. The heart of God is to lift up and edify the body of Christ, even in correction. Remember, we must always operate in love.

I said, "Brother, we are living in the time of Laodicea and all of us have to battle the spirit of Laodicea." I then quoted the third

---

[60] When a person enters in with such a vague request, it can be unsettling at first but immediately go to the Lord. In fact, before you begin praying for someone you should have already started seeking the Lord looking for direction even if you think you know what's wrong or they tell you what they think is wrong. In the situation I am describing, there was little time because there are usually people in line waiting to be prayed for; once one walks out, another walks right in. In other situations it is good to seek the Lord before you even speak to the person. For example, if you are in church and the Lord reveals a need to you, begin to pray and ask God what to do next and when. The when part is extremely important. After you have the full revelation and know all about it, then go to the person and ask them if you can pray for them.

chapter of *Revelation* where the church of Laodicea is described. The church age of Laodicea is the age of lukewarmness.

I said, "Brother, you have been fighting against the main spirit of this age, the spirit of lukewarmness, the spirit of laziness. This is what we all must fight against. This is where you have been having a hard time. This is the battle for this time and this age. We all must fight it. This is the Devil's main attack against us right now. I have a hard time fighting it at times too. This is where you have been falling. This is where your problem lies."

It was a hard saying but it was given in love, it was true, and it spoke to his heart. When a complete stranger can describe in detail exactly where you are in your spiritual walk, it shakes your world. It cracks you open, allowing you to even accept a hard word. It brings you to a place where you can change.

As I moved from the man to the woman I paused for a second and pondered what just happened. The fact that God will speak to us just like He did with the woman at the well still blows my mind. Even though that transfer of information from God to that man happened through me, as a vessel, it made me feel so small and God so big. I was just the littlest of tools sitting in God's tool box. God is so awesome.

Outside the tent a storm was forming above us. The clouds started to shift and the wind was picking up, forming a low howl.

As we moved to the girl, I was expecting another word from the Lord. It seems that most of the time what a person asks for is different than what they really need. Or many times there is a blockage that the person will not discuss because they are either too embarrassed or they are not even aware of it. It was different with this girl. I could see that she prayed a lot. Her request was exactly the heart of God. She asked for the exact thing that God wanted to give her.

I said, "You have asked for direction, you have asked to be able to see God's path before your feet and that is exactly God's heart. God is going to give you this thing but not the way that you expect."

I told her what God was showing me, "God is going to open your eyes to see the motivations of people's hearts to see why they are pulling you to and fro. People have been pulling you. People want you to do certain things. You feel pulled in too many different directions and you do not know which is the heart of the Lord. Now you will see the motivations of their hearts and see if they have

143

God's heart when they call you." She began to cry as we prayed for her to receive that blessing in fullness.

Another woman came in saying only that she had emotional problems. I did not know her and that is all she told me, nothing more. I began to pray softly, standing in front of her, again seeking God as to where this should go. Her face was quiet calm. She was not upset. She did not look "emotional."

What was the real problem God? What am I to say or pray for this unemotional "emotional" woman?

God spoke to my heart, "Trust me. Open your mouth and start to speak. I will put the words in your mouth."

Oh boy. Here we go. I was nervous to here that. Sometimes I have a hard time praying because I like to be in control and so does God. Here God was asking me to give up control and right away I was getting uncomfortable.

Shakily I opened my mouth and these words came out, "It is good that you have a man praying for you."

What?! Where did that come from!?!

It was not what I was thinking but it was what I said. I turned around and looked behind me as if someone behind me might of said it. No one was there.

Did those words actually come out of my mouth?

I turned back around and faced her again. I had to continue but where was this going?

The Lord was starting to speak, yet by all external appearances I was just some man speaking. On the outside, the flesh does not change. God was veiled in my flesh. I yielded more and allowed the Lord to speak again.[61]

All of a sudden it was as if I was watching from the outside. My perspective shifted. It was like I was watching my own body do things. It was like I was a spectator watching *me* minister to this woman.[62]

---

[61] Remember, God is a gentleman and will never force Himself on anyone. He will only go as far as you are willing to let Him. If I did not yield to Him, then He would not show himself. At any moment, even after I yielded, I could have taken back control. God only moves as you allow Him to move.

[62] In no way am I claiming that my spirit left my body because I am not sure about that. Actually I am still unsure of exactly what happened. All I can describe is what I experienced.

My mouth said, "You have had women pray for you many times concerning this grief that you carry and yet it always came back. Now it is good that you have a man praying for you. It is good because you have an internal barrier that must be removed. You have a barrier to fully receiving your healing. You have unforgiveness. A man hurt you emotionally in the past and you never forgave him."

The next thing that happened completely blew my mind. It was like I was on the outside watching my body do these things. Just then I saw myself do something that I would never have dared to do. Now I understood why the Lord needed to do it for me. I do not think that I could have brought myself to do this thing that my body was doing. That is why the Lord had to do it through me.

Holding both of the woman's hands, my eyes stared deeply into the woman's eyes. It was like I was a spectator in my own body; God was in control. I heard myself speaking in a soft voice, almost whispering, I said to the woman, "Now I will stand in for that man. In order for you to be free of this grief, you must forgive. If I stand in for that man and ask you to forgive me, do you think you will be able to do it?"

Tears rolled down her checks as she choked out, "Yes..."

In shock at what was happening I saw myself get down on my knees in front of her and beg her for forgiveness, saying, "I did something to hurt you. I did something to tear your precious heart apart and now I am asking you to forgive me."

The voice was soft and sweet. It was not my intonation. It was not my words. It was not how I normally speak. No way would I have done this. I saw myself stare up at her, eyes locked like magnets. I said, "I am asking for your forgiveness. Can you forgive me?"

I felt tears streaming down my own face yet it somehow didn't feel like it was my skin. I was in a bewildered amazement watching what the Lord was doing. Imagine the God of heaven, the great Creator of the entire universe on His knees begging someone to forgive only so that He could grant that person's freedom. Imagine the Lord of all creation lowering Himself to this level. What love! Isn't He wonderful!

Something broke deep inside of her as she cried out, "Oh, Yes! I forgive you!"

I felt a deep rush of pain exiting her body. It was like the opening of a dam. The stopped up river full of broken branches and green stagnant waters rushed out. She was set free. The pain left. The depression left. The guilt left. She was free.

All of a sudden it was me again. I was looking out of my own eyes up at her. I awkwardly and quickly stood up, feeling totally out of place in my own skin, completely uncomfortable being on my knees in front of a woman I didn't even know. She grabbed hold of me squeezing my rib cage in a great bear hug. I didn't know a woman could squeeze so hard! I was still in shock over what just happened and felt a little weird receiving the hug when it wasn't me at all, but in reality it is never me. It is always Him.

Expect it

In many places in previous chapters we have seen examples of God providing information to the person praying and so far in this book I have generically referred to this as *discernment*. This chapter on discernment discussing several aspects of this process of God providing us with information so that we might pray more effectively.

So then what is discernment? A strict definition of discernment is exactly the ability to know the spiritual source of a thing, to know whether or not a thing is from God, from man, or from a demonic source. Now that is the strict definition of discernment, but many people, including myself, use the term to more generally describe *all* of the ways God can provide information and we will continue with that convention for the rest of the book.

To be more exact there are several different gifts listed in the Bible that are informational such as the *word of wisdom*, the *word of knowledge*, and *discernment* among others.[63] God knows everything, even the very thoughts and the intents of our hearts and at times God will reveal these things to us when we are praying. God will give us information to help us do our job. The term I use to describe this in-

---

[63] In the twelfth chapter of 1st Corinthians Paul writes about the word of wisdom, word of knowledge, and discernment.

formation transfer is *discernment* although that is actually not the exact meaning of the word.[64]

Of course many may think, "Well, this discernment stuff is just something that God gives certain specific chosen and blessed individuals. Not everyone will be given spiritual knowledge when they pray."

Not so. Here is the complete truth. The person who is being called by God to pray must be granted all the facilities required to pray properly. God will not call us to do something without outfitting us with the necessary equipment to perform the task. God will not call us to pray for people without giving us information on how to proceed.

But can we be successful without it? Yes, but perhaps only to a limited level. I prayed for many years without the use of discernment only because I was unaware that it was promised. Glory to God, I felt fairly successful in praying because some were healed. During these times I often felt like I *knew* some small piece of information but I never spoke it out loud because of inexperience. I felt like I "had a hunch" but I never relied on that hunch because I didn't realize that it was God trying to tell me these things.[65] I thought that it was just my thoughts, guesses or natural intuition and perhaps at times it was. After a time I was enlightened to the fact that God always provides the tools for a job that He assigns. God will give us some form of discernment. Your form of discernment may not look exactly like mine, but God will always give us some form of an informational type of gift. God will provide us some form of communication so that we can complete the work. God will give us something far greater than thoughts, guesses or natural intuition. If we are called to pray for someone only once then it may only come that one time, but it will certainly come if we ask for it.

Now so far you may be thinking that this discernment is just a nice add-on feature, just like having power windows on your old

---

[64] In general I try to be as rigorous as possible with language and the exact meaning of words. Here I am being a little sloppy only because using the term *discernment* to describe all forms and manners of information that God can give us is a widely used convention.

[65] Even now I would not rely on a hunch, I only speak things that I know are completely from God. But back in those days it only felt like a hunch because it was an unopened, unwatered seed. It was not yet quickened by the Holy Spirit.

Chevy, something nice to have but not mandatory. Wrong! Jesus said that He would not pray without it and in fact when we shun discernment we are not following Jesus' example. In John 5:19-20, 30, it says:

> Jesus gave them this answer: "I tell you the truth, the Son can do nothing by Himself; He can do only what He sees His Father doing, because whatever the Father does the Son also does. For the Father loves the Son and shows Him all He does. Yes, to your amazement He will show Him even greater things than these."

> "By myself I can do nothing; I judge only as I hear, and My judgment is just, for I seek not to please Myself but Him who sent Me. "

Jesus would not pray for anyone without the guiding of the Holy Spirit. He did not move one step forward without some form of communication or information from the Father. He would do nothing unless the Father showed Him what to do first. Now I must repeat what I said earlier. If God is calling us to pray for someone, then God must give us some form of information. God must open up a method of communicating with us so we can see His will otherwise, like Jesus, we can and should do nothing. God will not leave us blind. If we are called to pray then we should expect some form of communication. God must grant us some form of discernment or, like Jesus, we should do nothing.

Discerning the Cause of the Sickness

One of the purposes of discernment when we pray is to allow us to see the root cause of the person's illness. There are many things that can be *roots* to the person's condition. We need to know *if* there is a spiritual root cause to the sickness and if there is one, what it is so that it can be pulled out. We do not want to cure the symptom while the cause remains. We want to pull out the root that led to the sickness or affliction. Sickness can not only be caused by virus or bacteria but also because of these roots. The Prophet David said:

> Before I was afflicted, I went astray.[66]

---

[66] David says this in Psalm 119:67.

And Psalm 107:17 says:
Fools because of their transgression and because of their iniquities are afflicted.

We sometimes must deal with the source of these roots such as transgression, iniquity, sin, unbelief or other causes before the person can receive healing. Of course it is not always the case that the sickness is caused by some form of curse or sin, sometimes they are just sick. It could just be a virus, bacteria, disease, genetics, or something else. In John 9:1-3, it is written:
And as Jesus passed by, He saw a man which was blind from his birth. And His disciples asked Him, saying, "Master, who did sin, this man, or his parents, that he was born blind?"
Jesus answered, "Neither has this man sinned, nor his parents: but that the works of God should be made manifest in him."

We should always try to discern the cause of the sickness before we pray. The last thing we want to do is free someone from a physical illness who is cursed because of sin. The Lord wants that sin taken care of first! If we do this then we just freed the person from the sign that was calling the person back to the Lord. We just actually did damage to the kingdom of God. Yes, they are not sick anymore so that is good, but what about the condition of their soul?

Discerning Blockages to Healing

A second reason for discernment is that it allows us to see things that might be blockages to people receiving their healing. Many people have hidden blockages to receiving healing such as bad teachings in their past which has lead them to not have faith or perhaps past experiences where praying has not worked the way that they expected.

Likewise, discernment can help us to see if what the person is requesting is what God actually wants worked on first. Many times people will want us to pray for one thing when God's priority is really something else *first*. In general I have found that when we follow God's priority, the things God asks us to pray for first many times ends up being either roots or blockages to what the person wanted dealt with anyway.

Unforgiveness

Of all the barriers to receiving healing, unforgiveness is the number one most common that can block a person from receiving healing in my humble opinion so let's spend some time on that one in particular.

So many people are bound up with past hurts. People have been wronged. People have been hurt and it is so hard to forgive. But you must forgive to receive. If we harbor unforgiveness in our hearts it has the potential to be a major blocker to our receiving healing. In Matthew 9:2-5, it is written:

And, behold, they brought to Him [Jesus] a man sick of the palsy, lying on a bed: and Jesus seeing their faith said unto the sick of the palsy; "Son, be of good cheer; your sins are forgiven."

And certain of the scribes said within themselves, "This man blasphemes."

And Jesus knowing their thoughts said, "Why is evil in your hearts? For whether it is easier, to say, 'Your sins are forgiven'; or to say, 'Arise, and walk?' "

When describing The Lord's Prayer, look at how much emphasis Jesus places on forgiving others. Matthew 6:8,12,14-15 reads:

Do not be like them: for your Father knows what things you have need of, before you ask Him.

And forgive us our debts, as we forgive our debtors.

For if you forgive men their trespasses, your heavenly Father will also forgive you:

But if you forgive not men their trespasses, neither will your Father forgive your trespasses.

In all clarity, Jesus explains the close link between forgiving others and having your own prayers answered in Mark 11:24-26:

Therefore I say unto you, what things so-ever you desire, when you pray, believe that you receive them, and you shall have them.

And when you stand praying, forgive, if you have ought against any: that your Father also which is in heaven may forgive you your trespasses.

But if you do not forgive, neither will your Father which is in heaven forgive your trespasses.

Discerning Answers to Questions

Another use for discernment is answering questions. There invariably comes a time in every person's life when they need an answer from God on a question that is important to them. Many people will come to prayer lines looking for an answer to a specific question. Perhaps, they want to know whether or not they should change jobs or move house. They may have relationship questions, financial questions, work questions, or family questions. Specific answers to these types of direct questions will not always be found in the Bible. The Bible does not say, "Jim, sell your house and move across state and you will be blessed," but God knows the entire future and can see all consequences of our actions. God can answer these informational questions. Here are a few examples.

When I was a new Christian, I was not so comfortable distinguishing God's voice from my own inner voice, the desires of my flesh, and the many external voices of the world and the evil influences, so I would pray in such a way that I could not be tricked or misled.

For example, once when I was unemployed I sent resumes to several hundred different companies across the country. I really did not care where I relocated; I was just desperate for a job and wanted to be where God wanted me to be. I had six interviews at different locations and two jobs looked very promising.

"What if I had two offers? How would I know which one was the one that God wanted me to take?" I thought.

I was not sure enough and I was afraid that I would choose wrong, so I prayed, "Lord, I have an important question and you know all things. I want to be where you want me to be and in a place that will be the greatest benefit for the kingdom of God, my family, and myself. Please Lord, let the company that you want me to work for make a job offer and the other company pull back their offer."

In this way, I would be guaranteed to be in the Will of God. In the end, one company pulled their offer and I was left with only one offer. God is good.

Now that I have been a Christian for a time, I sometimes pray differently. The way I just described was fine, this is just another way.

Some time ago, I again had the opportunity to change jobs, so here is how I prayed, "Lord, I have an important question and you know all things. I want to be where you want me to be and in a place that will be the greatest benefit for the kingdom of God, my family, and myself. I am asking you in complete faith that you will answer me. I am asking expecting you to give me an answer because you Word says, 'Ask and you will receive, seek and you will find' please tell me what you want me to do concerning this situation. "

Then I began to worship and thank Him for being such a great Father. I thanked Him because I knew that He would come and answer me. After a short time a *knowing* came upon my spirit. A spiritual revelation was given to me. [67]

The revelation did not come into my mind at all. It came completely into my spirit. This "knowing" was the Will of God and it was not placed in my head at all but directly into my spirit. There is a great difference between mental knowledge and a spiritual knowing and if you have never experienced it first hand that it may be as hard to understand as it is to explain. This communication from God was not a thought at all, it didn't come through my brain. It was a spiritual communication from God that came in on spiritual channels.

In this way, God communicated to me His Will. If I relied on Him telling me through my mind, I could be misled because evil spirits can also push thoughts into the mind or perhaps my own thoughts might confuse me. How could I tell the difference? This revelation did not come through my mind at all. It came into my spirit. This is a second way we can pray and expect to hear from God.

God will always answer questions in such a way as we know it can only be Him. Do not rely on a thought, a hunch, or a guess, expect God to make it real. We should always expect God to communicate with us.

When a person comes to be prayed for with a question it can be a bit unsettling. Praying for healing can feel easy in comparison because there is a strong Biblical framework. When a person comes in need of the answer to an earthshaking decision we must step cautiously. We should never fall into the trap of giving good advice and letting the person think that we are speaking for God. If the Lord does not show us anything then do not speak. Never be too afraid to say, "I don't know. The Lord didn't show me anything."

---

[67] Every Christian goes through times when they feel like they can't hear God's voice. I am no different.

Some time back two young ladies came to me, both with several questions about boyfriends, which colleges to attend, and other such things. They didn't want my advice; they wanted a word from the Lord God. The first one spoke then I prayed. After about five minutes I stopped and told her that I wasn't getting anything. I knew the Lord had her answer, but He wasn't telling it to me for some reason. She would have to wait or try something else. I refuse to just give good advice when a person is looking for an answer from the Lord. She could get good advice from anywhere; she didn't need me for that. I am not qualified to be a counselor anyway. I am not a social worker.

Then I turned to the second young lady and as I turned around in an instant I knew everything she needed. The Lord spoke this information into my spirit. It wasn't head knowledge. It was not a guess; I knew it because He showed it to me. She didn't even need to tell me why she was there. Before she opened her mouth, I told her why she was there and what she needed.[68] Then I answered all the questions that I had just spoken. It was so strange to my own ears! Where was all this coming from? It certainly wasn't from me. I would never dare to just say what I was thinking when it could affect the course of this teenage girl's entire life. Not only did the Lord tell her the answer to her questions, but He told her the questions too. There is no way I could know all this, it was all God. Even though I have heard it many times before, I was still as amazed as she was that God would speak like this.

I asked the two to stay in the prayer tent for a while, I felt like the work was not yet done for them. They stood on the side crying and holding each other for about a half hour while I prayed for a few other people. Perhaps there was something there that the Lord wanted the first girl to see. When I looked back at the first girl she was crying as she watched another young teenager give his life to God, accepting salvation. I felt led to go to her just then and just as I grabbed her hand, the Lord showed me her answer.

Timing

The Lord will show us many things as we walk in His will. The Lord will unveil things to us, even the very thoughts and intents of the heart. The Lord will show us how and why things have hap-

---

[68] She had different questions than the first girl.

pened to people and where the blockage is to receiving healing. But just because the Lord shows us a secret thing of someone's heart does not mean that we have permission to speak that information out loud and speak it right at that moment.

We must always have God's timing in what we do. Many times God will show us what is going on. If so, we should immediately pray, "Lord, do you want me to act?"

We should always find out if the Lord wants us to pray for a person directly or just to stay back and intercede. Many times the Lord will show us something and then someone else will pray. Afterwards we can give them a confirmation that we saw the same things.

There are other times where God will have several different people do different parts. We can be almost like actors on a stage. It is like God wearing the masks of our flesh and playing all the parts in the play. We should always ask God what and how much we are to say or do. Sometimes we will be told to just to say a few words and let others do the rest. Sometimes God will have us pray only after others have done their part.

Discernment is a vital and necessary part of our prayer arsenal. Expect it! Pray in faith that God give it to you. God must give us some type of informational gift. God must communicate with us. God is not going to send us out there blind.

Remember this is not about us anyway. We are not some type of psychologists who give out good advice then pray for people to be healed.[69] We are a prayer warriors! We should yield ourselves to God. If we are expecting God to provide all the power for the person to be healed then we should likewise expect Him to speak to the people in some way also. We should expect God to do *all* of the work through us.

Expect God to communicate to you. God called you to do a work; He is not going to leave you out there alone. God will give you the information you need to do the work. Let Him hold your hand. God will tell you where the hidden blockages are. God will reveal all you need to know to work through the problems. God will reveal to you the answers to the questions of the heart. Expect it.

---

[69] Well I am not a psychologist anyway. Maybe you are.

Chapter 10

Power

I was standing at the front of the auditorium with about fifty other people, fanned out, waiting to be prayed for. As the minister walked down the line and touched each person on the head or stomach they fell to the ground. A group of "catchers" followed behind the row of people.

As I glanced to the side, out of the corner of my eye, watching each one fall down in succession, I wondered if some were falling because they thought they were "supposed to." It was obviously expected. I do not know why but when they got to me nothing happened. My legs didn't get weak, I didn't feel any different, I just stood there and he moved on to the next person.

When I opened my eyes I was standing alone in the middle of the front of the rented hall, surrounded by a multitude of people on the ground. I couldn't leave as there were too many bodies in the way. I felt kind of embarrassed. I saw a few others who were not laying on the ground, but almost all were and I could tell that many were just laying there on the floor wondering what they were doing there. The lady next to me was laying on the floor with her eyes open, looking at me questioningly as if to say, "What in the world am I doing down here?"

I closed my eyes and prayed, "Well Lord, I am not going to fake anything. I am not here looking to impress anybody anyway. I am just here to worship You."

Then I started to praise Him softly.

In a quiet voice, I began to worship, saying, "Hallelujah."

As the whisper eased from my mouth, it suddenly erupted into a giant reverberation that carried itself through my whole body.

Wow! That was weird!

It was such a peculiar experience that I immediately opened my eyes to see if my body was actually physically shaking. No, nothing on my body moved or trembled; my hands were completely still. I felt like I was shivering yet my body wasn't actually moving! Weird!

As I continued to speak each new word of worship, they reverberated over and over throughout my body. They washed over me as if a smooth stone was thrown and hit the water of a calm, still lake. The waves did not seem to originate from my mouth, but from the center of my chest. It was as if I was speaking out of the center of my heart. All the hairs on my body began to stand at attention, confused as to why.

I do not know exactly why this was happening or what it meant but I began to feel different inside. My perspective was shifting, I was beginning to think differently. I was being changed inside. The reverberations were just a sign of something more, something deeper. God was working on me.

Others standing around had no idea what I was experiencing; I was just one of those who didn't go down when I was *supposed* to. The minister was coming back around, praying for the few who had not fallen yet. Obviously he thought that God wanted us on the floor.

By now many of the people who had previously fallen had gotten up and gone back to their seats. I still remained motionless and was praising in an almost inaudible voice, yet my spirit shook over and over with waves of a spirit-quake. As I stood there enraptured, caught up in the glory of God, suddenly lost to the rented hall around me, I was reminded of what had just happened a few weeks ago.

The anointing of the Holy Spirit had been very strong in the prayer tent on that day. Several people had types of anxiety or worry and asked for the peace that is promised in the Word of God. Jesus said that He would send the Comforter in the form of the Holy Spirit. These people cried out for God's Comforter. Proverbs 1:33 says:

> All who listen to Me shall live in peace and safety, unafraid.

When I prayed, I could feel the tension in their spirits. The Lord revealed it to me. As I prayed for the Lord's peace to enter into them, I could feel God's anointing well up inside me. My chest pushed out as if something inside was yearning to escape. It was like a river of living water that was flowing out of the center of my chest. It was the power of God.

I was so full of God's Rain that day. I don't know why but I was so full of God's living Water. I was a full vessel, so full of the Water of life. For some reason, God decided to use me on this day. The Water of God was pouring out of me! It was overflowing! It traveled down my arm like the blood flowing in my veins. The water was flowing, but it felt like it flowed on the inside! It was God's anointing power.

When I would start to feel it flowing out of me I would open my eyes and look at the person I was praying for. Most people would have their eyes closed so they did not know I was watching them. Right at the instant that I felt it flow out of my hand and into their bodies I could physically see God's peace flow into them and they were calmed, assured, and blessed. The sight blew me away. God allowed me to see His work first hand. I had a front row seat.

The peace I saw flow into them was not the peace of the world that leaves when there is trouble. This was God's peace. This was God's power. As time passes, false peace disappears. This peace was a rainbow on the edge of a cloud. It was spiritual peace. The tension would leave their shoulders and back. Tension left like stale air leaves a just released balloon.

God's vital, consecrating fire burned in them until it dissolved all anxiety and worry leaving a pure surge of an ocean of light. They breathed softer and slower. They were drenched in the delicate dew of the fresh fallen Rain. They were comforted by God. After a few minutes most would look up and broadly smile as they wiped fresh tears of joy from their eyes. It was not an "Oh, thank you for your time" smile, it was an authentic child-like smile of pure joy, freedom, and release. It was an "I have been truly touched by the almighty God" smile. I did not do anything, it had nothing to do with me, it was all God. It was God's anointing power.

Later I left the tent and went to the altar. I was just so happy inside to be a witness of God's power. Just to see it happen would have been enough for me, but God let me see it flow from my own hand! Why would he bless me so? The music was strong and powerful. A crowd was dancing feverishly. I wanted some of that. I wanted to dance before the Lord in victory. I wanted to celebrate what I just saw God do.

Just as I pressed through the thick crowd, a woman who was moving through the crowd and praying for people softly touched my shoulder without even looking at me. I had closed my eyes for a few moments and I barely felt her touch. All of a sudden my legs buckled and I felt myself falling down. I found myself resting on the soft earth, the side of my face pressed into some woman's sandal. It was the power of God.

After a time, I got up and finally made it to the front where everyone was dancing. I couldn't stop smiling. There was such a joy. I am not a dancer but I was dancing before the Lord. I felt such a freedom to just dance before God. Many others were on the floor, but at that time I didn't want to be there, I wanted to dance!

Just then, a man ran up to me, muttering some words, and aggressively grabbed my head with both of his hands. Apparently, he decided that I was going down whether I wanted to or not. I did not want to go down but he forced me down. I could tell that he wasn't going to give up so I let myself fall to the ground. I didn't want to wrestle with him in front of everyone and disrupt the meeting.

The anointing was just as strong down on the floor as when I was up dancing, so I laid there awhile. Maybe then he would leave me alone. Later, I got up and danced some more. There is no need to force a manifestation. The first time I fell it was all God. The second time it was all man. Yet, the anointing was still present. God still wanted to bless.

Later that evening, I saw some people praying for a demon-possessed woman near the rear of the park. She was twitching and shaking quite violently.

Then the Lord spoke to me.

I walked over and stood in front of her at a distance. Eyes closed tightly, her body shook fiercely. Her arms were spread wide and her head hung low, pointing at the ground like she was hanging on a cross. Her fingers curled backwards in an unnatural bend.

The Lord told me to breathe on her. From about five feet away, I exhaled, "Hooosh."

I didn't make much of a sound and the music and commotion throughout the place was loud. Certainly no one heard me or knew what I was doing, but as that breath of air came from my mouth she instantly stopped shaking and collapsed to the ground, motionless. She was set free. It was God's anointing power.

As I stood there in that rented hall, surrounded by bodies on the floor, thinking on those things that had happened those few weeks ago, the Lord started to speak to me. The reverberations continued to run through my body. Each shock-wave of anointing brought a deeper revelation. I started to see that *there is* a real manifestation. Why settle for imitation? There is a real power of God. There is no need to imitate what you see or try to force a person to the ground because you like to see people "slain in the spirit."

God is real and God manifests Himself in power. Do not try to force it, wait on Him. Do not imitate it, wait on Him. God will meet you and give you your own personal experience. God will touch you with a real power, not a fake imitation. God will put His power in you.

Quickening Power

It is clear that Jesus and the Apostles walked in powerful signs and wonders and that their message was vindicated by these signs. In fact, it was the signs that initially drew the people's attention. It was not so much Jesus' revolutionary message that made the people initially stand up and take notice but the signs and wonders.[70]

The power of God has a distinct purpose and God sends that power and those signs and wonders for a reason. One of the reasons God sends His power is because it is a proof that the message is true and that the Word comes from God. God's power is a vindication.[71]

John 10:25 says:

Jesus answered them, "I told you, and you didn't believe:

the works that I do in My Father's name, they bear witness of Me."[72]

This word *power* used here in the Bible is the word dunamis (δυναμις) in Greek. It is the root of the English words *dynamic, dynamite,* and *dynamo.* In the Bible it is often translated into English as *power, might, mighty, strength, virtue,* or *ability.* Dunamis refers to inherent power, power residing in a thing by virtue of its nature or power in action, what a person or thing exerts and puts forth.

---

[70] John 4:48

[71] Vindication means that it *provides proof.*

[72] Also see John 5:36

The power of God is the virtue that went out from Jesus when the woman touched His garment. It is actually the word dunamis. Jesus was saying that the woman pulled dunamis out of Him because of her faith. Mark 5:30 says:

> And Jesus, immediately knowing in Himself that virtue [dunamis] had gone out of Him, turned about in the crowd, and said, "Who touched my clothes?"

So this power of God, this dunamis, is given by God for a vindication, to prove that the message is sent from Him. Then if God is calling us to pray for people then He must also place power in us. If He gave us a message then He must vindicate and prove that the message is from Him by demonstration of His power. He must place in us something tangible, a portion of His power.

Paul tells us that it is God's power in us that allows us to minister. How can people be healed if there is no power? In Ephesians 3:7, Paul says:

> I became a minister by the gracious gift of God, which He gave me by the demonstration [effectual working] of His power.

Paul had signs, wonders, and demonstration of God's power. Then he goes on to say that it is this exact power, this dunamis, that *made* him a minister. Because he had God's power, then he could minister. It was having God's power that qualified him as a minister. He says, "I became a minister" due to the power, the dunamis, that God placed in him.

So then it is this power of God that we need to use. Paul even decries the act of convincing people with good rhetoric. Paul says his preaching was not with enticing words, but through the dynamic power, the dunamis, of signs and wonders by the Spirit of God. It was not special seminary training by man that empowered him. Paul was not full of man's power but God's power.

1st Corinthians 2:4 says:

> My message and my preaching were not with wise and persuasive words, but with demonstration of the Spirit's power.

More over, Paul says that it was the signs and wonders, the dunamis, God's power in action, that completed his preaching. In fact,

160

we could echo Paul's words that without signs and wonders, the gospel is not *fully* preached. Without signs and wonders, the gospel is only partially preached. The message is not complete.

Romans 15:19 says:
By the power of signs and miracles, through the power of the Spirit. So from Jerusalem all the way around to Illyricum, I have fully proclaimed the gospel of Christ.

According to Paul, the ministry of an Apostle is proven by signs, wonders, and deeds of dynamic power. It is the vindication of the calling. Conversely, how can a person claim to be an Apostle if there is no evidence? This can be extended to any ministry not only an Apostolic ministry. If God is calling you to do something for the kingdom of God then He will prove you also. Whatever God calls into being, God vindicates and proves with some supernatural sign. In 2nd Corinthians 12:12 Paul says:
The signs that prove me to be an Apostle: signs, wonders and miracles [deeds of the dynamic power, dunamis], were done in your presence, despite, what I had to endure.

Clearly, God's power is something that we desperately want and need. We see that without it we are not doing a complete job. Without it, we are not qualified by God. Without it we are not vindicated, we do not have God's sign –the symbol that we represent Him.
What we all want is God's power and more of it.

Life Force Power
The word dunamis as used in the Bible does not apply only to God's power, but also to the power found in all beings. It is the very life-force of a living creature. Dunamis is the force that makes a creature alive. Everything that is alive has some amount of dunamis. It is the power residing in a thing by virtue of its nature. All humans and living creatures have some amount of it.[73] It is their life force.
Angels also have a level of dunamis[74] and God has the great-

---

[73] 2nd Peter 2:11a

[74] 2nd Thessalonians 1:7

161

est dunamis. God is the source of all power and all life. The dynamic power of God that we seek is an attribute of God's nature and cannot be separated from Him. It is part of His nature. It is part of who He is. It is the life force of God, the essence of His Spirit. So in order to receive God's power, God's life must enter inside of us. Dunamis is not a description of an attribute; you cannot separate the power from the thing itself. If you remove the life from me, I will be dead. You cannot separate my dunamis from my body without killing me. Likewise, you cannot separate God's power from God. To receive God's power, the Holy Spirit must come inside of you. The dunamis of God comes into believers only through being filled by the Holy Ghost. In Acts 1:8, Jesus says:

> But you shall receive power [dunamis], after that the Holy Ghost is come upon you: and you shall be witnesses unto me both in Jerusalem, and in all Judaea, and in Samaria, and unto the uttermost part of the earth.

Once this dunamis of God enters inside, you will never be the same. It will change you and transform you. It is exactly this power that changes, transforms, and brings forth new life. That is the characteristic and purpose of this power, it is transformational. It was the dunamis of God that overshadowed Mary and placed life inside of her. Luke 1:35 says:

> And the angel answered and said unto her, "The Holy Ghost shall come upon you, and the power [dunamis] of the Highest shall overshadow you: therefore also that holy thing which shall be born of you shall be called the Son of God."

God's dunamis will transform your body. This is a transforming power, a power that brings life and light. It was exactly this dunamis that rose up Christ from the dead.[75] The transforming power of God's dunamis gave Sarah strength to conceive by the transformation of her body. Hebrews 11:11 says:

> Through faith also Sara herself received strength [dunamis] to conceive seed, and was delivered of a child when she was past age, because she judged Him faithful who had promised.

---

[75] Philippians 3:10

Dunamis is not limited to working in pastors, preachers, and priests alone. It is the dynamic strength of Christ in the inner man of all people. Ephesians 3:16-21 says:

That He would grant you, according to the riches of His glory, to be strengthened with might [dunamis] by His Spirit in the inner man;

That Christ may dwell in your hearts by faith; that you, being rooted and grounded in love, may be able to comprehend with all saints what is the breadth, and length, and depth, and height; and to know the love of Christ, which passes knowledge, that you might be filled with all the fullness of God.

Now unto Him [God] that is able to do exceeding abundantly above all that we ask or think, according to the power [dunamis] that works in us, unto him be glory in the church by Christ Jesus throughout all ages, world without end. Amen.

So this is the secret. This is the mystery. God empowers us to do mighty [dunamis filled] miracles by coming inside of us and doing them through us. He strengthens the inner man from the inside out then does something that we could not comprehend or even think of! It is "above all that we ask or think." This is the mystery; it is Christ in us doing the work. It is Christ with our flesh on. Colossians 1:26-29 says:

The secret, which He has set apart for himself [it is a hidden mystery] for generations and for ages, but now has been made manifest to the people, to whom God wanted to make known [it is revealed only to those elect of God, those who God chooses] how great is the glorious richness of this secret from among the Gentiles.

And the secret is this: The Messiah is united with you people!

In this rests your hope of glory. We for our part, proclaim Him; we warn, confront and teach everyone in all wisdom; so that we may present everyone as having reached the perfection, united with the Christ.

It is for this that I labor, striving with all energy, which works in me [powered] by His dynamic power.

Strength Made Perfect in Weakness

Every living thing, physical and spiritual, has a level of dunamis. God is the ultimate source of all dunamis as He is the very source of all life. In the quote above from Colossians 1:26-29, Paul says that we can come to a state of perfection when we unite with Christ. We can come to a fullness of power, a fullness of dunamis and reach a perfected state. So how do we do that?

It is much more than just getting filled with the Holy Spirit, although that is a big piece. Remember we all have some amount of power already. We all have some amount of natural human ability. One big factor in becoming perfected in godly power, is to make sure that our power is not of ourselves. We have to remain low. We do not do our work using our own power. We must continue to recognize that we are just shells. We are just earthen vessels that contain God's great power. 2nd Corinthians 4:7 says:

> But we have this treasure in earthen vessels, that the excellency of the power [dunamis] may be of God, and not of us.

This dunamis is the strength of God that is made perfect when coupled with the weakness of the flesh, since this power is made perfect in weakness. This is not to say that we should be sick. It is saying that we do not rely on our own strengths.

Paul was probably at least somewhat educated being a Roman citizen and a representative of the Pharisees but did not rely on the wisdom of man's words but on the power of God. Keep yourself humble! Do not rely on your own abilities. In 2nd Corinthians 12:9 Paul says:

> And He [God] said unto me, "My grace is sufficient for thee: for My strength is made perfect in weakness." Most gladly therefore will I rather glory in my weakness, that the power [dunamis] of Christ may rest upon me.

2nd Corinthians 13:4 tells us that Jesus followed this principle also. He kept his flesh weak and lowly thereby allowing the power of God to be strong in Him. He did not rely upon the strength of His flesh. It says:

> For though He [Jesus] was crucified through weakness, yet He lived by the power [dunamis] of God. For we also are weak in Him, but we shall live with Him by the power of

164

God.

Dunamis is the quickening dynamic power of the resurrection and the transformation of the body. This quickening dynamic power of God needs the dunamis of man to be humble and weak. God's power will be perfected when we rely on God's power and not on the dunamis of human ability.

To get full of this power we need more of the Holy Spirit and less of us. We need to grind away the flesh and get full of the Spirit. This is why I so emphasize certain things in the preparation section. These things that I have emphasized such as spending long periods of time in prayer and fasting are all things that grind away the flesh and bring the Holy Spirit in. Do things that starve the flesh and feed the spirit. Fasting of food, fasting of sleep, and fasting of time spent on the flesh grinds away the flesh. Feeding on the Word and feeding on the Spirit perfects the spirit.

God is full of light and life. God is full of dunamis-filled life force power and He wants to fill His children with this power. God wants to fill His children with His own life force, His dunamis. Get full of God's power.

Chapter 11

Faith is substance

It was late May, and I was three months in. I mastered learning how to swim faster than I thought I would, maybe because it was the one thing that most concerned me so it was the thing I put the most effort into. I was biking too. I rode my bike to and from work everyday, ten miles each way, and longer rides on the weekend. All in all, I was running about fifty miles, swimming about two miles, and biking about two-hundred miles per week. In retrospect, I was probably over-training *just a little* but something was burning inside of me and I couldn't stop it. It was controlling me. All I thought about was training. I even secretly fantasized that I might be able to win.

I was drawing in close on forty years-old. I had always heard about the mid-life crisis; the person who reached the big Four-O and all of a sudden realized that he was not where he thought he would be. He hadn't accomplished very many of his life goals so he becomes depressed because he thinks that his life has fallen into some sort of insignificance. I certainly wasn't there, but I was starting to feel a little older and slower. Somehow, someone put the idea in my head to participate in a triathlon. Don't know why I listened, I couldn't even swim. Why would I agree to such a thing?

Swim. Bike. Run. It sounded easy enough until I tried to put it all together. I had been an avid runner for over ten years so that was no problem but I only had six months to not only *learn how to swim* but get good enough at it to not drown over the half-mile open-water competition against prize-hungry weekend warriors. And then there was the bike ride of fifty or so miles in the middle. Why would I agree to such a thing?

I remember so distinctly how it happened. I got up that morning, got dressed, opened the garage door and pulled the bike out. The sun wouldn't begin to peek above the horizon for about fifteen more minutes so the sky was still in that hazy twilight of sunrise that I love. As I wheeled the bike out of the garage and leaned it against the stone wall next to my driveway, the cold crisp air smacked my face. It was definitely colder than normal, I could see my breath.

Its cold for April, I thought.

I had run an extra long fifteen miles the night before and was a bit tight. The rubber bands of my lower calves were bouncing, boing, boing, boing.

I was a little late rolling out of bed that morning so I had to pounce the pedals or I would be late for work. No time for my body to warm up! No time to stretch! For a moment I looked at the car and felt like I should just drive. I could make it with plenty of time to spare in the car.

Naah!

I jumped on the bike and slammed all my weight down as hard as I could. I was flying at twenty miles-an-hour in an instant. It wasn't even two hundred yards later when I heard it snap. It was an odd sort of muffled, rubbery sound, like stepping on a patch of leaves in the woods and snapping a branch deep underneath. Loud too. It didn't sound good. I winced as I tried not to think about what I just did: I partially tore my left Achilles tendon.[76]

Not knowing what had just happened I continued to pedal through the pain. At first it actually didn't hurt all that much anyway, in a few hours the pain would be excruciating.

By lunchtime, the back of the tendon swelled to about the size of a golf ball and I had excruciating flames of shooting pain firing up my leg. My entire calf muscle was trembling in constant spasms. It was only a huge bag of ice that helped me get through the day.

In the following days, I prayed to be healed but didn't seem to get anything. After each time praying my condition was the same and I didn't feel any faith rising up in me. I kept reaching down to feel it and it was always still there, no change, a huge golf ball-sized lump on the back of my leg, just above my shoe. I didn't know what was wrong with me but I couldn't seem to get past the pain.

---

[76] The Achilles tendon connects the calf muscle to the heel of the foot and when it is completely severed a person cannot even walk. I had a partial tear.

How can I believe I am healed when it hurts so much and the pain never goes away?

I prayed and prayed but the Lord was quiet. I couldn't seem to break through. Finally, in defeat, I made an appointment to see an orthopedic surgeon.

After several visits to different doctors, I had a special, custom made brace molded to my leg. I was supposed to keep the leg completely immobile so that it could heal on its own. The lead specialist told me that I could do nothing for six months. No biking, running or swimming. Nothing. I didn't need surgery but I had to give it time to heal on its own. Really I was supposed to walk as little as possible, he said.

I became so hard-headed and angry with the doctor. I refused to accept his diagnosis, I didn't want to hear it. This was too much for me. I was devastated. I loved to run, it always set me free. Before this triathlon craziness I was a runner. I ran to get alone; I ran to be free. I love the feeling of the air blowing past my ears when I am going all out, running as fast as I can. I love that feeling when it becomes effortless. It is like it is harder and harder to run faster and faster until I reach this inertia point, this point where I am actually running faster but it is all of a sudden easier, I am in my body's sweet spot. I love that spot and I didn't want to lose any of it.

After arguing with him for some time he surrendered, saying, "Well, obviously you are not going to do what I say anyway. I guess you can start swimming after three months, but if you do, I need you to not move that ankle. You have to immobilize it in the pool and I don't know how you are going to do that." He only allowed this much because of my hard-headedness. I stopped arguing with him and looked down at the white tile floor as I began to slowly realize the seriousness of my injury.

After I left the office, I decided to hunker down and pray for as long as it took. I was going to wait on God for the faith necessary for this miracle. I wanted that healing badly. I wanted my running back.

Then those old, familiar thoughts came. I have heard them all before. They came long, hard, relentless and non-stop.

You caused it yourself didn't you? You deserve all that pain that you are going through. You got stupid, trying to do something you shouldn't. You trained like you knew you shouldn't and now you think you can just pray it away? Now you want God to bail you out? How dare you to even ask!

I had to fight so many things; the guilt at my own stupidity. The victim mentality. The "you deserve it" mentality.

The problem was they were not lying this time. It was true; I did cause it. It was my fault. The blame was all mine. I was being selfish and distracted, lost in some absurd fantasy that if I only trained hard enough that I could somehow beat people who had been doing this all their lives. And for what? It was that stupid male ego.

God was trying to warn you and you ignored it! He was trying to tell you to drive to work and you ignored the warning! You had your chance, now you deserve to suffer. How can you ask God to help you when He was already trying and you didn't listen? Your own pride caused this. Don't you dare ask!

The voices always start with the truth before they twist it. It was true; God did try to warn me. Yet Jesus died for all sin. Jesus came to bring all freedom not just for people who think they deserve it. All have fallen short.[77] There is none that is righteous.[78] I never ask for healing based on whether or not it is deserved. I only ask based on God's promise and that sweet promise covers every situation and circumstance, no matter the cause.

I began to focus on faith. I had to believe. God responds only to faith. It is so hard to believe when the symptoms are staring us in the face. It is so hard to believe that we are healed when we have pain. I had tremendous throbbing pain; it never went away. It was hard to even sleep much less focus on believing that I was healed of this mess. But I had to believe. I had to have faith. God only respects faith. God only answers faith. The Bible say that without faith it is impossible to please God.[79]

I put on some soft praise music and shut myself in. I began to pray. I asked God to heal me then I praised Him and thanked Him for doing it. I was waiting on God. I was waiting for my doubts to leave. I was waiting for the faith that only God can provide.

---

[77] Romans 3:23

[78] Romans 3:10

[79] Hebrews 11:6

Five minutes turned into fifteen. I continued to pray and worship. It seemed like I was rising up. I started to feel a little taller like I was elevated in my viewpoint. At first it was so hard to keep focused as my mind kept drifting back to the pain, so I got more desperate and pushed harder.

Just keep focusing on Jesus, I told myself.

Fifteen minutes turned into forty-five. I felt like I was floating as I stood there in my living room, praising God. I was drifting in this hazy place of God's holy presence. I felt like God was all in the room, all around me and in me. He was everywhere. I was floating in a cloud of God's glory.

Floating in the hazy goodness of a caramel-coated swirly something-something

All of a sudden,

I feel

Right

The clouds, the clouds

Little fluffy clouds

Puffy and fluffy, little fluffy clouds

Right

Pushing past the now to a place of eternity where everything and everywhere and all in all is simultaneously just there and all in sync with all that was and is and it's just like it feels like it's just a pause into silence

Right

Air blowing through every

Single

Strand

Of the hair

In my

brain **Right**

Reaching out for a transcendent reality that is all of a sudden all around me like I don't know where it came from but it's here and

171

it's now and it's nice and it's smooth and it's all around like right now in this kind of a place

        and

              I feel

Right

Time melting into time to go beyond to

                        No time

Floating on the nothingness

Like everything is so soft and so airy
Like swimming in some kind of a swirling milk-chocolaty goodness that is oh so real and oh so right and oh so I can feel it going all through me

              Yeah

Right

Sunshine and light beam down on me

                  Beam down, beam down

                          beam down on me!

Cause He's here and now

                 and

                      The tingling

                            Wow!

My skin is full of a symphony of raised hairs and goosey bumps all up and down

              All up and down

        Right

To oneness

              To the one

                    One

I just kept praising and praising, and focusing on Jesus. I wasn't asking Him for anything. I wasn't focusing on anything but Him, just spending time with Him. Just being alone with God, drifting in His presence.

After about an hour or so I realized that I hadn't felt the pain in a while. I had been so enraptured with God in some kind of intoxicating hazy place of His presence that I forgot about everything else. I forgot about the concerns of my ankle. The pain was completely gone.

I bent down to feel it and the bump was just as large as it had been —just like a golf ball, yet it did not hurt one little bit! Wow!

The following two days, I prayed the same way. I prayed until the glory came. I prayed until I stopped focusing on my symptoms. I got my mind out of the way and focused completely on Jesus. On the second day, after over an hour of worship, the swelling shrunk by about half and the final day I was completely healed and my ankle was back to normal. The Lord God accomplished in three hours of worship what the doctor said should have taken six months.

Two weeks later I ran a 13.1 mile half-marathon in Delaware without a problem.[80] The week after I had my follow-up visit with the doctor and he had trouble keeping his eyeballs in his head. He couldn't stop smiling as he bounced around the room saying, "I don't know what you have done, but *no one* heals like this!"

I started to say, "Well I pray and..."

Cutting my words in the air, he jumped up and started shaking his pointed finger in the air, saying, "Well you keep doing that, because it obviously works!"

What is Faith?

Now we will return to the discussion on faith that we started in earlier chapters. As a person that is going to be praying for others, it is good to have a firm foundation in *exactly* how faith is developed not only for your own knowledge and understanding but also because some people you pray for will respond better when you teach them how faith works when you pray for them. Although not everyone

---

[80] This was during the Delaware Marathon Running Festival. A few people who knew of my injury started screaming at me to stop running when they saw me on the course and I couldn't stop laughing.

needs this. Many people do not need to be shown "how it works." Just show them the scriptures in the Bible, they take God at His Word and believe it, and then the person receives the healing. Some others cannot seem to believe anything unless they understand the mechanics behind it. They have to know "how it works" in order to use it.

Everyone has something that will help them to believe. Everyone has a certain mustard seed. Find out what their mustard seed is and give it to them. All you need to give them is that little bit of faith, that little mustard seed, and you will see the mighty hand of God. Faith is the necessary element in this work and everyone has something that will help them to unlock their faith. God responds only to faith. We must help them to gain faith. In Matthew 9:29, Jesus says:

> Then he touched their eyes and said, "According to your faith will it be done to you."

Matthew 13:58 says:
> And He did not do many miracles there because of their lack of faith.

In Luke 17:6, Jesus says:
> He replied, "If you have faith as small as a mustard seed, you can say to this mulberry tree, 'Be uprooted and planted in the sea,' and it will obey you."[81]

In previous chapters we gave a very brief scriptural basis for healing and looked briefly at the mechanics of faith and how faith is developed. Remember, the approach to healing is always through faith. We said that obtaining spiritual faith is a process. First, a person has to hear about the thing they are to believe in. Second, the person must make a mental choice to accept what they heard as true. Third, the Holy Spirit must come and reveal it to the spirit. The Holy Spirit must provide the faith. Hebrews 2:2a says:
> Looking unto Jesus, the author and finisher of our faith.

---

[81] Here are a few more references that show that God responds to faith: Matthew 9:2; Matthew 9:22; Matthew 15:28; Matthew 21:21; and Mark 10:52.

But what exactly *is* faith? There are people who claim, "What I confess; I possess" meaning that if they claim something *in faith* then God will grant it.

Unfortunately, there are many who do not understand exactly what faith is and are not claiming in faith but are claiming *in hope*. We need to know exactly what faith is if we are to use it properly.

So many take faith to mean something that they cannot perceive with their five senses yet something that they want so badly and ask God to give them. They do something physically, they take action, they step out "in faith", yet this is not faith at all.

Let's say, for example, that a woman wants something so desperately –maybe she is in a wheel chair and wants to be healed, she hears the message that healing is promised and she wants it so badly. A glimmer of light shines, there is a twinkle in her eyes.

Maybe God will give this to me! she thinks.

She steps out "in faith" and tries to stand up.

Many times people in this condition don't have enough faith to cure a hangnail yet God will honor them at times or perhaps God will honor the faith of those around the person who are praying and at times they will be healed. What they are operating in is hope. But we want much more than that. We want a true Holy Ghost filled faith that can move mountains. So what exactly *is* faith?

2nd Corinthians 4:13 says:

And since we have the same spirit of faith, according to what is written, "I believed and therefore I spoke," we also believe and therefore speak.

There is no problem with people speaking "in faith." I do it all the time. But what we want is to speak in true faith, not in hope. Notice in the quote above that they speak after they believed, after they have obtained the faith. They are not speaking in hope, or speaking to try to convince themselves. They are not saying what they want God to do; they are speaking out what they already know. After they have the faith, then they speak. So what exactly *is* faith?

Faith is Substance

Hebrews 11:1 says:

Now faith is the substance of things hoped for, the evidence of things not seen.

175

Faith is substance —it is something tangible. It is substantially real. It is not physically tangible but it is spiritually tangible. It actually is *something* in the spirit world. It is a substance. Just as we have a spirit and our spirit is actually something in the spirit world, so is faith something spiritually tangible. Our own spirit has spiritual substance. Faith has a spiritual substance. It is something that is actually real.

When you have faith for something you actually have something tangible inside of you. You are in possession of something spiritual. Faith is like a piece of spiritual something. It is like a chunk of spirit.

Faith is not a concept. Faith is not an idea. Faith is not something we hold in our mind. Faith is not hope. Faith is not a thought. Faith is something tangible; faith is substance.

For you to receive that substance, that faith, God must give it to you. Faith is not something that comes into your mind through reasoning or much studying. Faith is not something that comes by being mentally convinced.[82] Faith is something spiritually tangible and can only be given by the Holy Spirit. Hebrews 2:2a says:
Looking unto Jesus, the author and finisher of our faith.

Acts 3:16 says:
By faith in the name of Jesus, this man whom you see and know was made strong. It is Jesus' name and the faith that comes through Him that has given this complete healing to him, as you can all see.

Romans 12:3 says:
For by the grace given me I say to every one of you: Do not think of yourself more highly than you ought, but rather think of yourself with sober judgment, in accordance with the measure of faith God has given you.

The Apostles obviously believed Jesus to be the source of faith and even asked Him to provide them more. Luke 17:5 says:

---

[82] We spoke of mentally convincing people using the scriptures of the Bible in early chapters, but remember that all we were attempting to do there is convince their minds so that they might make a choice to believe.

176

The Apostles said to the Lord, "Increase our faith!"

Jesus is the provider of faith. In order to receive faith, God has to come and actually place it inside of us or else we do not have it. Faith is substance and God's Spirit comes and gives us this spiritual gift. It is something that we actually have. When God provides us with faith, it is like Him actually going inside of our spirit and attaching a chunk of faith to our spirit. It becomes a part of us. It becomes a part of who we are.

God provides our faith. We can never "believe" enough mentally. We must have a spiritual faith and God alone provides that faith. Believing in our mind is not faith at all but just thinking. Faith is something spiritual and is in our spirit. Jesus is the author of all faith. God provides faith through the work of the Holy Spirit and there is no amount of thinking alone that will work. It is through faith and faith alone that miracles happen.

Here is one example of how faith works. Let's say that a person wants to be healed to rise up out of his wheelchair. The man sits through your sermon and you read him scripture after scripture that describes healing and you show him that it is promised for him. You are mentally convincing the man that he should expect to be healed if he asks God for it.

At some point he goes out on a limb and chooses to accept it. He mentally makes a choice that what you said is true and he wants to try to trust God. What he is actually doing, spiritually speaking, is choosing to open up his spirit to receive faith from God. No matter how much you mentally convince this man, it will still be only in his mind without the power of the Holy Spirit. God alone provides faith. Until the Holy Spirit comes and binds that faith to his spirit, all he has is something mental. It is not yet faith.

When that man chooses to believe that promise of God he is actually opening up his spirit to God. He is getting his mind "out of the way" and yielding himself to the moving of the Holy Spirit. This is where the real war takes place! So many reach this point and don't move forward!

He is opening himself up to the Holy Spirit to come and drive that spiritual truth deep into his spirit. He is opening himself up so that God can bind that truth to his spirit. Remember faith is substance; it is something spiritually tangible. It is something that we actually have. God must come and provide it.

177

Once the man has reached that point, he must wait on God to provide the faith. The Holy Spirit will come and provide the wheelchair bound man the faith and once that happens nothing can keep him in that chair. A knowing will fall upon him. A supernatural, spiritual faith will be bonded to his spirit, changing him. No matter his condition or what others say, he will *know in his spirit* that he is healed because he will have a spiritual faith substance inside. His flesh will have no choice but to respond.

When we operate in faith, we are not moving out and doing things or speaking things based upon hope or based upon something that we *want*. We already know it deep down in our spirit because it has already been attached to our spirit by God. It is something that has already become a part of us. When we have faith for something, we have something tangible, bound to our spirit. Following the Apostle's example, first we must have faith and then we speak.

Faith, Hope, and Healing

I want to further illustrate the difference between hope and faith using a story.

When I was a child, there was a small corner store called Mato's that many of the neighborhood kids would visit to buy candy. It was actually a family's home in which they converted the living room into a small convenience store with a small candy counter.

At times my Dad would give me a few coins after doing my house chores and I would straight-away run down to Mato's to visit his candy counter. My father didn't always give me the coins, but I always had to do the chores. I always hoped that I would get some coins, but they didn't always appear.

While I was working cutting the grass or helping him clean the garage or basement, I hoped that I would get some coins. Sometimes I did, sometimes I didn't. Of course, my Dad was a good, caring and loving father and I might have been 99.9% sure that he would give me some coins, if he had them, but until the coins were actually in my possession, I was still only in hope. I did not yet have a 100% guarantee that the candy was mine.

Once he handed me those coins, it was just as good as already having the candy. Before I had the money in my possession, I hoped I might get some candy. Once I had the coins, I knew I was going to receive some candy. The money was not the candy, I couldn't eat the money, but to me it was just as good. I had the faith that the candy was mine. No matter if there was something blocking my path to Mato's corner store; I had the substance that proved that the candy was mine. I had the evidence in my hand that proved that the candy was mine. I had the purchasing power for the candy.

Yet I still had to walk down to the store and pick it up. What I had before I had the money was hope. Once I had the money, I had faith. Now that the coins are in my possession, I have all authority to walk down to that store and buy the candy. Now I can step boldly down the street knowing that I will receive some candy upon presenting Mr. Mato with my coins. That candy is mine. I own that candy and I am going to go claim it.

With faith we actually have something tangible. It is substance. Just like the coins to buy the candy, we have something real that we own. It is a part of us and God provided it to us. It is not hope! No matter our symptoms or our physical condition, when we have faith we know that the healing is ours. We have a faith inside of us that is part of our spirit and no matter the physical condition on the outside; we have the proof-positive guarantee that the healing is ours. We have the evidence deep inside of us that what we had once hoped for is real. The symptoms of the disease may still be in our body but we know, spiritually, without a shadow of a doubt, that we are healed. We might not have seen the least bit of change in our physical condition, in fact we may feel physically worse at times, but we know that we are healed and no one can convince us otherwise.

There is no doubt whatsoever; it is something spiritual that has been bound to our spirit. It is something real that has changed in our spirit. Not to downplay hope, because hope is so necessary, but hope is not a substance. Hope is good and necessary, and it is good to have hope, but faith is something entirely different and entirely more.

Faith is like that handful of coins that was given to me by my father. It was real and substantial; it was the purchasing power of that candy. It was the guarantee that the candy was mine. It erased any shadow of a doubt that I might have had. The candy was mine. Faith is something real and spiritually tangible given by our spiritual Father that He puts inside of us and binds to our spirit. Faith is real and substantial; it is the purchasing power for healing. It is the guarantee that the healing is ours.

179

Once we have that spiritual substance inside of us, we become different. It changes us. We now feel so bold and confident to step forward and claim our blessing. It is not even a question. When I had the coins I went straight-away to Mato's to claim my candy. There wasn't any doubt that the candy was mine. Once we have the faith we can go straight-away to claim our healing. We have the authority to claim it. We have the purchasing power. We have the substance; We have the evidence. We have the faith.

The Layers of Man

Here is one more illustration on how the process of faith works to help better explain how we obtain faith.

The human being is composed of a spirit, a soul, and a body and we can look at these different aspects of the human being as layers in order to help explain how God plants this faith inside of us. 1st Thessalonians 5:23 says:

And the very God of peace sanctify you wholly; and I pray God your whole spirit, and soul, and body be preserved blameless unto the coming of our Lord Jesus Christ.

Paul uses the Greek word πνευμα (pneuma) to mean spirit, Ψυχη (psyche) to mean soul, and σομα (soma) to mean body.

As an illustration to further explain how faith is developed let's look at man as layers. In our illustration, on the innermost layer is the spirit of man, encompassed about by his or her mind and finally surrounded by his or her flesh.[83] Now for God to plant a seed of faith deep in our spirit, He must first penetrate the outer two layers. He must first breach the physical layer of the flesh (ears, hearing) and then the soul layer of the mind (psyche) in order to finally reach the spirit. God is spirit and everything significant that He does is in the spirit. In order for a person to receive true Holy Spirit-filled faith, the person must have that spiritual piece of faith from God bonded to their spirit. Yet for this to happen, God must first cross these two barriers of the flesh and the mind.

---

[83] I am only using this as an illustration; I do not say that we are exactly like this.

Remember, God is a gentleman and will not force anything on anyone. If you are not open and willing to accept what He has to offer then He will not force it upon you. So then, each individual must open themselves up physically, mentally, and spiritually to God's Spirit. They must open up these layers to Him. As we said in the first chapters, they must hear with their ears (body layer) and choose to accept it with their minds (soul layer) before God can plant the seed of faith in the spirit.

Let's look at a Biblical illustration to describe these layers of man and the process of obtaining faith. In Mark 4:3-8, 13-20 Jesus tells the famous parable of the sower:

"Listen! A farmer went out to sow his seed. As he was scattering the seed, some fell along the path, and the birds came and ate it up. Some fell on rocky places, where it did not have much soil. It sprang up quickly, because the soil was shallow. But when the sun came up, the plants were scorched, and they withered because they had no root. Other seed fell among thorns, which grew up and choked the plants, so that they did not bear grain. Still other seed fell on good soil. It came up, grew and produced a crop, multiplying thirty, sixty, or even a hundred times."

Then Jesus said to them, "Don't you understand this parable? How then will you understand any parable? The farmer sows the word. Some people are like seed along the path, where the word is sown. As soon as they hear it, Satan comes and takes away the word that was sown in them.

Others, like seed sown on rocky places, hear the word and at once receive it with joy. But since they have no root, they last only a short time. When trouble or persecution comes because of the word, they quickly fall away.

Still others, like seed sown among thorns, hear the word; but the worries of this life, the deceitfulness of wealth and the desires for other things come in and choke the word, making it unfruitful.

Others, like seed sown on good soil, hear the word, accept it, and produce a crop—thirty, sixty or even a hundred times what was sown."

So in this parable, the seed that is sown is the Word. Again, it is not just something you hear, it is something spiritually tangible that is sown into the spirit of man just like the seed of a plant is placed in the earth.

The various descriptions of the different types of soil are examples of different types of people who have all accepted God's seed, the Word, to different levels of depth. The seed has penetrated to different layers using our analogy.

In the case of the first type of person, the soil that is along the path, the seed never penetrates the mind because the soil is hard packed. They refuse to even consider it. They heard it with their ears so it penetrates the body layer but they reject it with their minds.

In the case of the second type of person, the rocky soil, the seed penetrates into the soil but it doesn't go in very deep. The seed does not develop any roots. They have heard the word with their ears and have even accepted it in their mind, but have not yet fully opened themselves up to something spiritual. They are in that dangerous place of holding something in their mind that they as yet do not truly believe in their spirit. There remains some shadow of a doubt. It has not yet been planted in their spirits so they do not yet have faith. They only have some mental conception in their minds, they only have thoughts. They as yet have not *fully* made a choice. Remember, God is a gentleman and respects our will. God will not force anything upon us that we have not already accepted. We have to accept it *completely*. We have to erase all shadows of doubt from our minds. In this second case, the spirit-filled word of God penetrates the second layer of man, the mind, but does not penetrate the third layer, the spirit. They only have a mental conception.

The final two examples are both good soil. They both receive the word, the seed, that tangible piece of faith in their spirits. That spiritual portion of God is heard with their ears, accepted by their mind, and penetrates to the very depths of their spirit. The seed takes root in them. It changes them. The seed is something tangible, it has substance. It is actually *something*. It is a tangible piece of spirit from almighty God that has been placed deep inside their spirit that grows and takes root. It is the Word. It is seed.

But notice that although the third type of person, the thorny, weed-filled ground, *does* grow a full-grown plant, yet because the worldly weeds were not removed, they are choked and do not bear fruit. They did not act upon the faith that was placed inside of them. They had the faith but did not take authority over those foul weeds but just let them lie there, choking the Word. The plant had roots

182

meaning that they had faith. The Holy Spirit sowed that spiritually tangible faith-seed into the depths of their spirit and it grew. But the plant did not yet produce fruit; there was no supernatural manifestation because they did not act.

Finally, the fourth type of person, who is called good soil, hears the Word physically. They accept the Word mentally; choosing to accept it as truth in their minds. God binds that faith to their spirits; they receive a supernatural faith. It is something tangible and real that is placed deep inside of their spirit. No matter the outside conditions, the person knows what the result will be. Having this faith, they act upon it in all boldness and confidence. They act upon that faith and they produce a crop. They produce supernatural fruit because the seed that was sown was supernatural.

If we are to pray for people with results, we must become masters at helping people to get their mind "out of the way" and false ideas out. We must become masters at showing them and teaching them the Word concerning healing so that their mind might accept it. We must learn to recognize and discern the difference between a person truly believing and having spiritual faith and a person who says that he or she believes yet it is all mental thinking.

As prayer warriors we want people to be healed physically, mentally and spiritually. To receive any of these great blessings from God the person we are praying for has to believe; we have to help them to believe.

This world is full of all sorts of people; some will be full of faith and just need someone to pray with them in agreement, we can let our faith join with their faith so they can receive.

Others will already know the scriptures and have a pretty good mental conception but just need that extra little push to receive the faith that only God can provide. Help them to get rid of that last shadow of doubt so that the Holy Spirit can come and provide faith. Pray for the faith to come.

Still others will not know much and will come forward in hope that their situation will change. Find out if they know the Word and show them the Word. Show them the promises of God concerning their situation. Find out if they can accept the Bible as the Word of God. Everyone has a mustard seed.

We should pray for anyone; not only those who go to our churches. We should never limit ourselves to praying only for Christians. Jesus didn't limit himself that way!

183

I have seen God heal all types of people with all manners of faith and levels of belief. I have seen notable miracles done to people who were not even sure if they could believe in Jesus. But they believed afterwards. Remember that Jesus healed many that did not yet believe that He was Messiah. The Bible calls Abraham the father of faith when he was yet uncircumcised. Jesus was sent to the unbelievers, not to the high priests. One of the methods of bringing in the unbelievers was His mighty miracles. So often I have seen Christians that will only pray for other Christians because they think that they are "believers." God is sending us to shine our light in the dark places, not where there is already light. We must become masters of praying for people who need to learn and accept faith.

We must completely understand faith and be able to discern our own heart and where we stand. We must make sure our faith is secure before we step out and act. And once that faith is solid we must not hesitate! Once we have that internal knowing deep in our spirit, we must proceed with all boldness and authority and we will have a great harvest!

Chapter 12

Authority

It's Saturday evening and the Holy Spirit's strong. Two teen-agers are just giving their lives to the Lord as an old guy in worn-gray dungarees tearfully rededicates himself to a Christian walk and another man, excitedly demonstrating his healing of an old shoulder injury, swings his arm around like a golf club. The music's anointed in a surreal kind of way and the skies are wonderfully, almost mag-nificently clear; it's a good day to be a servant of God. I smile in wonder at the sense of victory in the air; it's coming soo easy.

I'm standing near the north side of the park just to the left of the musicians belting out contemporary gospel when a stiff ocean breeze unexpectedly cools my left cheek. Large, dark, storm clouds approximately ten to twelve miles off appear at the edge of the hori-zon, just south-eastward from us. There is an unusual thickness to them. Thick and dark, not gray but black, they seem bloated and awkward like a pregnant woman who is two weeks past-due, stum-bling to keep her balance. Lightning pummels the ground below as if all the clouds' anger is focused on some distant, small village. Fac-ing the still far-off storm, threatening gusts of wind begin to push my hair back and I think, "I don't like this." The wind suddenly howls in my ears, speaking to me, telling me, "I am coming to get you. I am coming to destroy your little revival meeting."

Wondering if my eyes are deceiving me, I tilt my head back and look up at the sky directly above and see that fleeting clouds are also moving east to west, directly across our path. Our clear cloud-less sky is being invaded by quick moving clouds clearly telling me that it's not only the wind blowing at ground level but also high in the sky as well; it's not an illusion, the storm that is seemingly creep-ing up out of nowhere is heading directly toward us.

Standing in contemplation, staring at my new enemy, I can't understand what's happening as the dark and ominous storm clouds creep closer and closer, fade darker and darker, and bellow louder and louder. Every few seconds another flash reaches out from the angry darkness. The crowd becomes suddenly aware of the storm in the distance as the air swirls and becomes more turbulent. The people are still somewhat calm for now, but not too happy about it. A mother nervously calls her children closer and another family is folding up their chairs.

For some reason I know those clouds don't carry a light, wispy kind of rain but a deep, heavy soaking rain, a rain that hefts its weight around like an old west desperado when it pushes into the room, wryly smiling as he blocks the cantina entrance, eyeing his next target among the simple town-folk. Thinking back, I remember recently being caught out in my backyard, out by the shed, when a cloud opened up with a punishingly heavy rain. Soaked through in a moment, sopping wet, the weight of the heavy rain coursed down my face and off my chin. I felt like all that rain chose me, singled me out. *Ha! I got you!* I felt like I was the sole reason for that tiny cloud opening up. A few yards away it was completely dry. That is the kind of flash-flood August rains we sometimes have around here.

As I stare at the now pitch-black clouds belching constant lightning, a good brother comes up behind me and whispers, "You know I hate to say this, because I know you put a lot of work into this, but if that storm comes any closer, you are going to have to shut this down for the safety of the people."

Of course what he said is completely reasonable. The safety of the people comes first. The storm is heading directly toward us. We have a generator with electrical equipment out in the middle of an open field. There are musical instruments, lights, amplifiers, and thick cables strung out all over the place. We are going to be rained on and potentially could be threatened by lightning. There are families with children here. Many walked in from the surrounding area and have little or no shelter. The park is basically all open with little cover at all. We have to keep them safe and we can't let the equipment be destroyed by the rain. It's not even our equipment.

A peculiar road put me in this uncomfortable place and I am all of a sudden wondering what I am doing here. It's my first outdoor revival meeting and I am definitely out of my comfort zone.

"It was the last thing on my mind to try to organize this thing," I think, "No way did I want to do this -but I felt the call so strong. Did I hear right? I think I felt like it was God I remember that I felt like I absolutely had to do this maybe I didn't hear right maybe I am just being set-up why would God call me to do this so that it could be destroyed did He really call me?"

As the wind pushes me back, I move my right foot behind for support as I lose myself in thoughts of how I came to be standing in this suddenly terrible place, "I was stretched tremendously in the six months of preparation leading up to this moment so many things happened with so many people pulling in different directions but finally we gained coordination of seven local churches with prayer preaching and music to be held in three different parks over three days with all seven churches giving and doing different parts on different days but now the storm is coming and it is all going to be destroyed this is all on my head why did I organize this thing is this God's will those clouds couldn't be God he wouldn't call for so much work and then destroy it no way maybe I didn't hear right maybe the devil tricked me oh I wish I wasn't here everyone is looking to me to make a decision on *what to do!"*

In upset frustration I think of all the hard work that has gone on to bring us to this point, *"We just started! It's the beginning of the first day! Why?"*

It was a long, slow road to get here but now everything is happening super-fast and accelerating faster and faster. I'm not afraid; there's not enough time for that. I'm just trying to keep my mind caught up with everything all around me. It's like I'm suddenly at the center of a vortex, spinning and spinning. The clouds are heading directly at us and the wind is pressing. It suddenly becomes a stiff, constant wind. The cheap tarps strung over thin metal poles shake and shudder, but the musicians consciously try to ignore it. The storm is now about five miles off but it feels oh-so-much closer.

I say nothing to that brother. I mean, what could I say? I open my mouth but nothing comes out. I don't know what to do but I know what I certainly don't want to do, right now I don't even want to be here.

My thoughts can't get away from the frustration because I just can't understand why this is happening, "We are just getting off the ground the Spirit's just starting to flow openly the glory of God is falling and people are getting healed saved and delivered no way do I want to shut this down but the ugly black clouds are coming, the rain is coming, the lightning is coming!"

There is nothing else I can think to do but pray, "Lord, you placed me on this path. You told me to do this and there is a storm blocking my path. Lord, there is an angry storm blocking me from accomplishing what you have called me to do."

I don't feel weak or threatened, my heart's not melting, but yes, I am upset. I have to admit that to myself. I'm frustrated, but one thing I still know is true: I was called. God called me to this, I reassure myself. It was one of the strongest words I have ever felt in my entire life. God called me to this, this is my assignment. God placed me on this path I tell myself. I am in God's will doing God's work. It's God's problem, not mine. I am doing what He told me to do. He is going to have to deal with this. I pray in protest, "God, I know you wouldn't call me to do this and then let it be destroyed!"

Finally, I fully give it over to Him, "Lord, this is your revival, not mine. You need to handle this. I can't do it!"

Suddenly, reassurance rises up in me. It really just rises up. I don't know where it comes from but it feels like faith is rising and I suddenly know that He really wanted me here. God placed me on this path. The path I am on is God-ordained. I know that I am in God's will.

Just then another brother comes up and stands next to me facing the storm. The wind pushes the three of us back and I squint my eyes as tears blow directly back into my hair. As the three of us stare at it, one of them asks, "What are you going to do?"

God speaks to the secret place of my heart saying, "Speak to the storm."

All of a sudden this unnaturally intense focus falls on me and it's as if everything else around me disappears. I don't formulate a plan of attack, I just unconsciously start doing it. I begin to pray out loud and command the storm to move. I sway my arms in giant full-bodied arcs as if I am pushing the storm across the river, in the direction of Delaware. Not asking nicely, not hoping, I somehow know deep down that the storm has no choice but to obey. With such a complete and intense focus I don't even realize that I am still standing toward the front where everyone can see. How ridiculous I must look! One of the two chuckles and walks off a few paces while the other joins me in taking authority over the wind. We pray and push. We're two fools swaying our arms at the air like two lost Indians dancing a rain-dance trying to foolishly control the uncontrollable, uneducated to the true nature of science and the world around them. We would look comical if the situation wasn't so pathetic.

Suddenly the unexplainable happens. The flapping tarps stop flapping. The people pause from gathering their children and belongings and look up at the sky. The stiff breeze suddenly calms. It becomes incredibly calm —unnaturally calm compared with all the wind and noise before. The air suddenly falls to our feet, dead and unmoving like a bird hit by a car, dying an instant and forgotten death. There is such stillness to the air that all the hairs on my body stand on end and I become suddenly conscious of my own skin. The crowd is collectively holding its breath and suddenly, simultaneously, decides to exhale. The wind changes direction. The clouds are beginning to move sideways someone points out excitedly. It's over. It's gone. The direction of the storm really changes. The storm heads in the exact direction that we were pushing it. The storm goes to Delaware.

I look up amazed to see a clear circle of cloudless sky open above us. The storm left so quickly, it was almost like it was never there. I feel like I am in a car-crash, mental shock, half-daze of awe-struck amazement, *"Did that just really happen?"* Turning back, I see a rainbow over the back of the city, behind us, and I wonder when it first appeared, still not able to put this all together in my mind.

The following morning I see a local news report that describes a bizarre and unnatural phenomenon of some storm clouds mysteriously and dramatically changing direction and moving against the prevailing wind in Delaware.

It makes me laugh.

What is Authority?

A person in authority has both control over a situation and the responsibility for the results of that situation. That person is responsible for the outcome and responsible for commanding those things that concern the situation. God gives us a portion of His authority and expects us to use it and holds us responsible for *how* we use it. This chapter will draw out the subtle differences between God's authority and man's authority and further show that when we operate in

189

God's authority we are really ambassadors of God carrying out His will.

Authority of Man and Authority of God

There is an authority of man and an authority of God. The authority of man is derived from the individual's behavior. A person can speak well, loudly, or boldly and some would say that he "speaks with authority." This is what we will call *man's authority* and the authority of God is nothing like that. When we speak using God's authority we are speaking as a representative of God. We are speaking as an ambassador or an envoy. We are speaking as one *sent* from God.

Having God's Authority is not just having an authoritative sounding voice. True godly authority is derived not from the manner in which a person speaks but who the person is. If a particular person's voice sounds strong and commanding and there is no weakness or shakiness to it, then that is good but that is not the same as speaking in God's authority. When you speak with God's authority, you could whisper but things will happen because it is not about the timber or resonance of your voice but that God has sent you and you are representing Him; you are operating using His authority.

Notice that the authority of a commander over his soldiers is similar to God's authority in Matthew 8:8-10. The commander does not have to scream at his soldiers but only *tells them*. His authority is not derived from the way that he says it but who he is:

> The centurion replied, "Lord, I do not deserve to have you come under my roof. But just say the word, and my servant will be healed. For I myself am a man under authority, with soldiers under me. I tell this one, 'Go,' and he goes; and that one, 'Come,' and he comes. I say to my servant, 'Do this,' and he does it."
>
> When Jesus heard this, He was astonished and said to those following Him, "I tell you the truth, I have not found anyone in Israel with such great faith."

Man's authority is not only given due to the sound of a person's voice but also many other qualifications such as education level, financial income, or personal appearance, among others. Although there is nothing wrong with having any or all of these, they have nothing to do with having God's authority. In fact, Jesus purposefully chose Apostles who were not highly educated Pharisees. He chose commoners to show us that these qualifications were not important. God will give His authority to whom He will.

Mark 1:22 says:
The people were amazed at His [Jesus'] teaching, because He taught them as one who had authority, not as the teachers of the law.[84]

God has authority based upon who He is and God grants us a portion of that authority to carry out His will. We are not *little gods*, but are ambassadors for Christ. When we walk in God's authority we are acting as His representatives and acting with His authority, doing things that He commanded us to do. In Mark 6:7,12 Jesus gives authority to the Apostles:
Calling the Twelve, He [Jesus] sent them out two by two and gave them authority over evil spirits. They went out and preached that people should repent. They drove out many demons and anointed many sick people with oil and healed them.

Authority in the Will
When God gives authority, it is not authority to do our own will but to carry out His will. Too many people think that when they become Christians that they can just command or pray for things to happen that they want. They neglect to go to Father first and ask Him what His will is. They run out and start praying or trying to command things to happen then later, when those same things do not happen, they are baffled as to why. Well, because it is not about what we want, but what God wants.
John 13:19-20a, 30 says:
Jesus gave them this answer: "I tell you the truth, the Son can do nothing by Himself; He can do only what He sees His Father doing, because whatever the Father does the Son also does. For the Father loves the Son and shows Him all He does."

---

[84] Also see Matthew 7:28-29

"By myself I can do nothing; I judge only as I hear, and My judgment is just, for I seek not to please Myself but Him who sent Me."

It is always about His will. He gives us authority, but it is authority to carry out His will. We know that we are in His will because He provides the faith for the work. The authority comes through faith. It comes after we have faith. Remember 2nd Corinthians 4:13 says:

And since we have the same spirit of faith, according to what is written, "I believed and therefore I spoke," we also believe and therefore speak.

First we need the faith, the knowing, that seed of spiritual something that is planted deep inside of us by the Holy Spirit. Then we speak. We act. We move and speak with authority. Once we have the faith then we have all authority to stand up and claim the blessing. We have the authority to speak.

First pray and ask God to heal the person. Wait until the revelation strikes that all necessary blockages have been taken care of. Wait until the revelation strikes that *it is done*. Wait until the revelation strikes that a mustard seed of faith has been planted. We have the green light. We have the "all go," then floor the gas pedal and move with all authority. Then command the sickness to flee. Then command the demons to leave. Then command the body to be whole. It is the Holy Spirit provided faith that provides the green light to speak in authority. Without it we are like the Apostles in Matthew 17:14-20:

When they came to the crowd, a man approached Jesus and knelt before him. "Lord, have mercy on my son," he said. "He has seizures and is suffering greatly. He often falls into the fire or into the water. I brought him to your disciples, but they could not heal him."

"O unbelieving and perverse generation," Jesus replied, "how long shall I stay with you? How long shall I put up with you? Bring the boy here to Me." Jesus rebuked the demon, and it came out of the boy, and he was healed from that moment.

Then the disciples came to Jesus in private and asked, "Why couldn't we drive it out?"

> He replied, "Because you have so little faith.[85] I tell you the truth, if you have faith as small as a mustard seed, you can say to this mountain, 'Move from here to there' and it will move. Nothing will be impossible for you (NIV)

The Apostles were trying to do right. They were compassionate for the people, trying to help them receive healing but they were speaking out of order. They were trying to speak *in authority* when they did not yet have faith. Get the faith first, then speak.

Our authority must be in line with God's will. Jesus said in our previous quote that if we have faith as mustard seed, then we can command mountains to move. But notice the qualifier, we must first have the faith in order to speak with authority. We cannot speak what we *want* God to do and expect mountains to move. Only speak after the faith rises up for it.

In the true story at the beginning of this chapter we commanded a storm to change direction and it certainly obeyed us. Yet, I have no authority to walk outside and command the winds right now at this particular moment. It is not God's will for me to do it and even if I tried it would not happen. The faith is not there for it because it is not God's will and God provides faith. So if it is not God's will then we will not be provided the faith and we should not speak.

Let me further illustrate this concept with a story. When I first answered the call to pray for others I was concerned about my inexperience so I went to God seeking some practice. I looked for any inconsequential opportunity to pray. I wanted to practice where it wasn't important so I could learn how to pray properly. I was trying to build myself up so that when the time came to pray for a person's needs I would be ready. I remember distinctly sitting in my backyard and trying to command sticks, twigs, and branches to move *with authority*. No matter how hard I bellowed my voice the sticks did not move. I tried to make my voice a bit deeper, to make it sound more authoritative, but that didn't work either. Speaking with God's authority is not about having an authoritative sounding voice or speaking in such a certain tone or manner that makes people mentally think that you are in charge.

---

[85] The New King James translation says: "Because of your unbelief"

On another occasion I was on my daily run along the edge of a busy road when a small squirrel darted into the oncoming traffic and was killed. I saw the whole thing, it happened fifty feet in front of me. No one stopped their vehicles; it was just an insignificant squirrel.

As I ran up to his dead body, I stopped and began to pray. I asked God to raise the squirrel from the dead. I figured that it was of no consequence and this would help my faith to grow. Nothing happened. I stayed there for over a half-hour and nothing happened. I did not even feel the slightest bit of faith either.

I could have stood there for years and nothing would have happened because I was not acting in God's will. It was not that I didn't wait long enough. It was not that I didn't pray hard enough. It wasn't my educational background, the clothes I was wearing, or the sound of my voice. I was attempting to accomplish my will not God's will.

Actually these experiences made me down, but it was good in a way because it caused me to seek the Lord in order to obtain a deeper understanding and revelation on these principles. What we need to move mountains is to speak with the authority of God. In order to speak with God's authority we first need faith and faith is only supplied by the Holy Spirit. Seek the Father and His will and you will see mountains move.

Authority over your own possessions

So we need to be in God's will but do not let that statement paralyze you into inaction. When we pray for someone for healing, we do not have to go to God and ask if the healing is promised, we already know it is promised through the scriptures. We can confirm with God to see if there is some blockage or something that is spiritually more important that He wants dealt with first, but the healing itself is already promised and already ours. We do not have to seek God to see if it is His will to heal.[86]

Likewise, many other things are promised in the Word that we do not have to ask for such as the authority of teaching or of laying on of hands for receiving the Holy Spirit. We have the authority

---

[86] Matthew 10:1

to influence others by the edification and teaching.[87] We have the authority to lay on hands to receive the Holy Spirit.[88] These are things that are promises of God. We have that authority already. The Bible is full of promises and they are all ours to claim.

But remember, God wants to heal the whole person, spirit, soul, and body and in that order. As we have already said, God's priority is to heal the spirit first, then the soul, then the body. First find out if there is anything God wants worked on first, then the other forms of healing will come more easily.

Taking Action on Faith

In other situations that are not clearly promised in the Bible, we simply need to ask God what is His will and He will tell us. He will provide the faith. The authority that we have is always based upon God providing us faith to do the work. We are using God's authority, we are His representative. So we need His faith *before* we take authority.

Once we have the requisite faith, we are not done. We must take action. We must stand in authority and command the demon to leave. We must stand in authority and command the sickness to flee. We must stand in authority and command the flesh to be whole. It is not enough to just ask God. He expects us, as prayer warriors, to take authority over these things. Remember our discussion of the four types of soil in the parable of the sower in the previous chapter. We looked at Mark 4:3-8, 13-20, but here is a selected verse:

> Still others, like seed sown among thorns, hear the word; but the worries of this life, the deceitfulness of wealth and the desires for other things come in and choke the word, making it unfruitful.
>
> Others, like seed sown on good soil, hear the word, accept it, and produce a crop—thirty, sixty or even a hundred times what was sown."

These two are both good soil. They both receive the Word, the seed, that tangible piece of faith in their spirits. That spiritual seed is heard with their ears, accepted by their mind, and penetrates to the

---

[87] 2 Corinthians 10:8; 13:10

[88] Acts 8:17-19

very depths of their spirit. The seed takes root in them. It changes them. But the third type of ground did not act upon the faith that was placed inside of him. He had the faith but did not take authority over those foul weeds but just let them lie there, choking the Word. The Holy Spirit sowed that spiritually tangible faith seed into the depths of his spirit and it grew. But there was no supernatural manifestation of healing because he did not act.

Conversely, the fourth type, who is called good soil, not only receives the faith but acts upon it. No matter the outside conditions, he knows what the result will be. Having this faith, he acts upon it in all boldness and confidence. He acts upon that faith and produces a crop, producing supernatural fruit.

The third type of ground had a seed sown into his spirit which grew roots and even a plant but did not produce a crop because he did not act. It is like having faith but not acting on that faith. Once we have faith we must act or there will be no crop. Without action, there will be no fruit, no supernatural manifestation, no healing, and no miracles. James 2:14-26 says:

> What good is it, my brothers, if a man claims to have faith but has no deeds? Can such faith save him? Suppose a brother or sister is without clothes and daily food.
>
> If one of you says to him, "Go, I wish you well; keep warm and well fed," but does nothing about his physical needs, what good is it?
>
> In the same way, faith by itself, if it is not accompanied by action, is dead.
>
> But someone will say, "You have faith; I have deeds."
>
> Show me your faith without deeds, and I will show you my faith by what I do.
>
> You foolish man, do you want evidence that faith without deeds is useless?
>
> 22 You see that his [Abraham's] faith and his actions were working together, and his faith was made complete by what he did.
>
> 24 You see that a person is justified by what he does and not by faith alone.
>
> 26 As the body without the spirit is dead, so faith without deeds is dead.

This quote starts out using the example of feeding and clothing the poor so that is what many have focused on when talking about "works." Yet, this passage is so much deeper. It is about so much more than just homeless outreach and feeding the poor. It is about taking action when God provides faith for a work. Once God provides the faith, we must step out and act or else the faith is wasted. We can have so much faith, yet if we do not act in authority on that faith then it is dead. It does not bear fruit.

We must take action. We must take authority once we have that faith. It is the action that makes faith complete. If we do not take action then our tree might as well have been dead because it is not producing fruit. If we do not act on the faith then we might as well never had it. If we do not act on the faith then the faith is unfruitful. If we do not act on the faith then the faith is useless. It is the action that makes faith complete. Faith without action is dead.

Humbleness

A final word on authority is about humbleness. Once we have taken authority over a sickness and the person is healed, we must be so careful as to not take credit or think that we did anything. God could have chosen to use a burning bush, a bright shining light, or a donkey, but He chose us. [89] We are no more than vessels that God flowed through. God did all in all. Yes, it is such a blessing to be identified with the Creator, but the credit is always all His.

God is calling us to use His authority in boldness yet we must still be humble. God calls us to step forward in boldness, to stand in the face of the storms, to stand boldly and take on whatever is thrown at us and He will be at our side. Yet, at the same time, we are asked to be a humble people.

For example, when praying for a person, you might use God's authority that He has given saying, "Demon of cancer, I cast you out by the authority given me by the Lord Jesus Christ. I cast you out in the Name of the Lord Jesus Christ."

It is you casting it out, but you are using God's authority that He gave you. Then Jesus grants freedom. The healed man feels a

---

[89] Exodus 3:2 describes God in a burning bush. Acts 9:3 describes God in a bright shining light. 2nd Peter 2:16 and Numbers 22:28-30 describes God speaking through a donkey.

release. The tormentor leaves and the pain leaves. God's peace enters into him. Then something dangerous might happen. The person opens his eyes, lifts his head and looks at you. He thanks you. This is where the danger steps in.

God blessed by allowing that healed person to look up at you, and that is such a blessing that it will make you cry at times but never allow yourself to think that you had anything to do with it. It is all God's work. It is all for God's glory. We might speak with all boldness and God's authority and yet we must remain humble for we are merely channels of God's power. 2nd Corinthians 4:5-7 says:

> We are not preaching about ourselves. Our message is that Jesus Christ is Lord. He also sent us to be your servants. The Scriptures say, "God commanded light to shine in the dark." Now God is shining in our hearts to let you know that His glory is seen in Jesus Christ. We are like clay jars in which this treasure is stored. The real power comes from God and not from us.

conclusion

The information in this book may be new and exciting for some of you and not so new for others. For some, this information could be almost overwhelming. You might feel like you do not know where to begin. Others might feel disqualified because you now see where you fall short or might not feel like you can do anything until you have mastered some aspect of one of the teachings. Please do not think like that. Understand that the devil may come and try to bind you up telling you that you cannot pray until you have some aspect of what you have read.

Do not listen to his lies. Start with what you have now. We all have to start somewhere. No matter how much you read and how much you think that you know, you will not have a true and deep understanding of these principles until you get out there and start doing them. When the Holy Spirit starts pulling on you to pray, step out and do it! No matter if the confidence you feel in yourself is weak, go out and do it. Pray and give out as much as you have and let God handle the rest. This is how we all begin. Actually this is how I operate even today.

Let grace cover the rest. God will cover you and teach you at each step. Understand that you will never be complete of yourself anyway. No matter how much you know and how confident you feel, God will always use every opportunity to stretch you. You will always be learning.

Never underestimate the power and will of God to stretch you farther and teach you more even as you pray for people. The Lord knows what you are capable of and where you need to learn and grow. He will let you learn as you pray and also learn where you make missteps. Yet even with your missteps, God will still complete the work. Trust Him.

God will teach you something at the same time that you pray for the needs of people and this never stops. Almost every time you pray for someone God will stretch you. Even though God is feeding that person you are praying for through you He will be still teaching you new things and reaffirming past lessons.

It never becomes easy. People can put their brain on autopilot when working on easy, repetitive tasks. Driving to work every morning, I sometimes pull into the parking lot and wonder how I got there. My brain was shut off, I did not have to focus and concentrate to drive that road. Being a prayer warrior is never like that. Even if it is something that you have prayed for many times, God will do something different in order to educate you. Expect to be stretched every time.

You Can Do It

God is good. God is faithful. God is trustworthy. We have an awesome God. We have a supernatural God. You are going to see some supernatural things happening. Sit down and hold on because the ride is about to start. Put your seat belts on and strap in because you are about to take off.

Plan for it. Expect it. Ask God what He is doing in your life. Seek God for the changes He is making in your heart. Don't look for others to do what God is calling *you* to do. God doesn't want it all to come through one person or one group. My God is a God of diversity and a God of plenty. God is looking for prayer warriors to rise up all over the world.

This book was written to equip and strengthen you. This book was written to encourage you that you can do it! God has put it in you. I can't put it in you. This book can't put it in you. God has already done it and God is calling it out. He is calling it forth. You can do it. God wouldn't put something in you unless He wanted it to be used. He put His power in you for a reason. He put it in you before you were formed. Your role is to discover it, to seek God for the revelation of it. Your role is to start functioning in it once you have discovered it. Your role is to grow in it once you have been functioning in it. You can do it!

This book is only to help you. This book is to come along side of you and help you to move forth in what God has already called you to do. Every one of us is a part of the whole and every part is important. Every part has to be healthy for the whole body to be healthy. God is calling us to come together as a body and for every one to fulfill their part. He is calling each of us into our part of the body. No one can do it for you. No one can do the thing that God has called you to do exactly in the way that God called you to do it. He is trying to use you to do it.

Expect God to do things in your individual life. You are so necessary for this body! Our God is a supernatural God. Expect a supernatural God to do supernatural things in your life.

Father, in Jesus' name I stand before You in proxy for all the prayer warriors who are now stepping into the new boots that You have provided them. I stand before You in faith that, as they step in, You would nurture and protect. Some of them step in willingly, some step in cautiously and questioningly, but they are stepping in Father. Watch over them dear Lord. We know you are a God who saves. You are a God full of love who moves on behalf of His children out of love. Lord, we recognize that it was only through Your great love that we can even be reconciled to you. And even more sweet Jesus, so great is the mystery that You would do so much more, that You would actually put Your great, wonderful, holy, and perfect Spirit within us. This is so incredible!

We thank you dear God for we are unworthy and it is only through faith and under the blood of Jesus that we become worthy of such honor. Lord we are so willing to receive and understand the power of Your love. Thank You for providing the priceless treasure of Your love.

Every time You move dear God, the devil tries to block, thwart, and side track. So as the devil tries to attack your children, Father I ask you to move as no other can move. You Word says that when the enemy comes in like a flood that You would raise a standard. Lord I ask you to raise up Your standard. Raise Your victory flag for Your children. Let the world look, see, and marvel at Your glory.

No one can plan like You can plan. No one can turn things around like You can, Father. Turn the Devil's attacks into victories.

Almighty Father, I ask You to bless greatly. Father, look down upon the hearts of your prayer warriors. Look down upon Your children and lead them in the work that You have called them into.

Lord Jesus, I ask You to glorify Yourself through them. Rise up prayer warriors to glorify Your name.

Father, I call in a full manifestation of Your plan and purpose for this day. Let nothing hinder Your work.

Lord, I ask you to protect what you are doing in these lives, place protection upon these ministries.

Father, I call for Your revelation to strike the hearts of Your people; deal with Your people. I call blessings down upon your people. Release a spirit of love in the hearts of your people.

Lord, I ask You to continue to anoint and bless Your people and Your work. Lead Your people into perfection.

We give you all honor, glory, and praise and ask these things in the wonderful, beloved, and holy name of the Lord Jesus Christ.

Amen.

About the Author

James Cardona received his degree in Religious Studies from the University of Delaware. He also attends and prays at Harvest Time Worship Center in Salem, New Jersey and resides in close-by Pennsville.

Mainly operating in the church's prayer ministry, James prays for people whenever he is given the opportunity. Additionally, he works in prayer tent ministry at outreach events such as food banks, food pantries, clothing and food outdoor outreaches for the poor and homeless, along with revival outreaches, both at his church and events sponsored by other churches in the Southern New Jersey area.

Contact James from his website at:
WWW.jamescardona.ORG

Also you can read his weekly blog at: **jamescardona.wordpress.com** where you will find testimonies of divine healing along with other inspirational material.

Also by James Cardona

The Indwelling:
An Introduction to a New Relationship with God

ISBN: 978-0-6151-3668-4   116 pages, 6"x9"

Salvation is a process. A new believer is not born again into a perfect state of being. Once a person accepts salvation and the saving blood of Jesus Christ, they are only taking the first step on a long journey. The walk with God is a walk of change and development. The walk with God is a walk toward perfection as believers grows into the image of sons and daughters of God.

Too many people stop after the first step. Too many people stop after giving their lives to Jesus, being baptized with water, or receiving some form of confidence that they will go to heaven. There is so much more! Do not stop! This book shows the path to a higher plane, a higher walk.

Using direct references from the Bible and true personal stories, this book provides the necessary knowledge to receive the Baptism of the Holy Spirit and maintain a Filling of the Holy Spirit. Read this book to find out how!

God will only take you as high as you are willing to go. It is up to you. This book shows you the differences between these different steps or levels and the benefits of attaining a higher level. There is a closer walk with God, the indwelling of the Spirit, and it is available to you right now.

2828370R00107

Printed in Great Britain
by Amazon.co.uk, Ltd.,
Marston Gate.